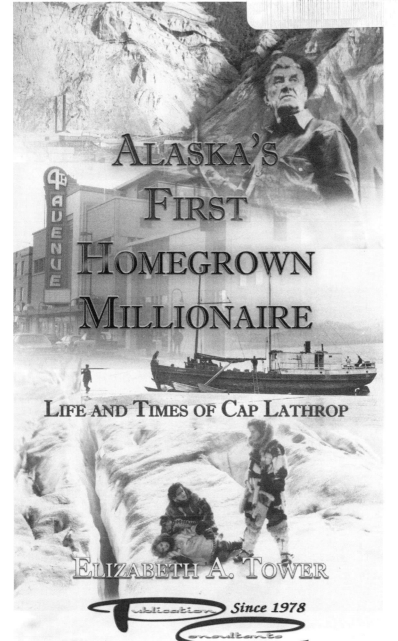

ALASKA'S
FIRST
HOMEGROWN
MILLIONAIRE

LIFE AND TIMES OF CAP LATHROP

ELIZABETH A. TOWER

Publication Consultants *Since 1978*

PO Box 221974 Anchorage, Alaska 99522-1974

ISBN 978-1-59433-039-1

Library of Congress Catalog Card Number: 2005911398

ACKNOWLEDGEMENTS

The author wishes to thank Miriam Dickey Kinsey, Mr. and Mrs. Austin Cooley, Alvin O. Bramstedt, Mr. and Mrs. August Hiebert, Mr. and Mrs. Albert Swalling and Robert Atwood for their cooperation and encouragement in the preparation of this book, which was originally published in 1990 under the title of *Mining Media Movies*. I was fortunate to have been able to interview these people, some of whom are no longer living, at that time.

Table of Contents

ACKNOWLEDGEMENTS   3
AUTHOR'S PREFACE   5
THE CAPTAIN'S CHOICE   6
PUGET SOUND — 1889-1895
    A Fortune Made and Lost   8
TURNAGAIN ARM — 1896-1900
    Captain of the *L.J. Perry*   *11*
VALDEZ AND COAL BAY — 1901-1908
    Oil and Marriage Don't Mix   21
CORDOVA — 1909-1914
    A New City to Build   30
ANCHORAGE — 1915-1921
    Movie Magnate of the Empress Theatres   40
THE CHEECHAKOS — 1922-1924
    Alaska's Home-Grown Motion Picture   50
HEALY RIVER — 1925-1931
    A Coal Mine Pays Off   63
CORDOVA — 1932-1936
    New Industry for the Copper City   70
FAIRBANKS — 1937-1941
    KFAR — Key For Alaska's Riches   78
WORLD WAR II — 1942-1947   86
POLITICS — 1946-1949
    The New Deal Comes to Alaska   95
DEATH AND TAXATION — 1950
    Statehood Drive Continues   106
END OF AN EMPIRE — 1951-1958
    Ice Palace and Statehood   114
ENDNOTES   120
BIBLIOGRAPHY   124
INDEX   125

AUTHOR'S PREFACE

Cap Lathrop died four years before my husband and I came to Alaska in 1954. His name was still well-known in Anchorage because the Lathrop Company owned a local radio station and two theaters. Like many young people who settled in the territory after World War II, we enthusiastically joined the statehood movement with our new-found friends. They told us that Lathrop had been a leader of the anti-statehood forces.

Several years later we heard that Edna Ferber was in Alaska gathering material for a new novel that would help the statehood cause. When we read *Ice Palace* in 1958, we cheered Thor Storm, the statehood advocate, and booed "Czar" Kennedy, the exploiter patterned after Cap Lathrop. *Ice Palace* helped Alaska win statehood and then drifted into obscurity, to be resurrected briefly in a movie, starring Richard Burton as the scheming "Czar."

Fifty years later, few Alaskans can tell their teen-agers why Lathrop High School is so named. The Fourth Avenue Theater in Anchorage and the Lacey Street Theater in Fairbanks still stand, but have been converted to other uses.

This is the story of Cap Lathrop who built these theaters — and a lot more. Readers can decide whether to remember him as the exploiter pictured in *Ice Palace*, or as a builder of modern Alaska.

Elizabeth A. Tower
Anchorage, Alaska
October 2005

THE CAPTAIN'S CHOICE

Alaska was the biggest choice that Austin Eugene "Cap" Lathrop made in his 84 years. While others took their fortunes south, Lathrop chose to stay and invest in Alaska. During half a century in the far northern territory he tried, and usually succeeded, in a variety of enterprises that helped to assure Alaska's readiness to become a full-fledged member of the United States. He captained a steam schooner; drilled for oil; hauled freight; built apartments and theaters; started banks and radio stations; published a newspaper; served as a city mayor, a state legislator, a university regent, and Republican national committeeman; established a model salmon cannery; developed Alaska's most successful coal mine; and produced a motion picture. So diverse were his activities that each half decade of his long life provides a new story in Alaska's development.

Cap Lathrop lived frugally and amassed a large personal fortune which he invested in making Alaska a place in which other people could live comfortably. Having no immediate family, he considered all Alaskans to be his family. Alaskans called him their "first home-grown millionaire."

Lathrop was a man of contrasts, which became increasingly apparent as he grew older. His gruff manner scared some people while his warmth charmed many. Parsimonious to a fault in small matters, like supplying adequate electric light bulbs, he gave generously to charitable organizations. Although frequently dressed in old "bush" clothes, he insisted on using up-to-date quality material in all of his buildings. He provided motion picture entertainment for the entire state, but rarely watched a complete film. He built luxury apartments in Cordova, Anchorage and Fairbanks, but had no real home of his own. Lathrop was in the forefront of development in construction, transportation, communication, seafood processing, banking and mining, but was slow to recognize the potential for statehood in Alaska. While protesting that Alaska was not ready to assume the financial burden of statehood during the 1940s, he busied himself building the infrastructure that facilitated statehood ten years later. Cap was happiest when doing hard physical work. His final wish, "to die with his boots on", was fulfilled on July 26, 1950, when he died in a Healy River coal mine accident. Cap left assets worth millions, but his personal belongings would scarcely fill a flight bag.

PUGET SOUND — 1889-1895
A Fortune Made and Lost

Timing was the secret of Austin Lathrop's success. Early in life he learned to recognize and capitalize on opportunity. Fires still burned in Seattle, Washington on June 7, 1889, when Lathrop, a husky dark-haired farm boy from Ashland, Wisconsin, boarded a train for the northwest to make his fortune out of the ashes. He had never before left his close-knit family, but had the blessing of his father, who foresaw that his young son's skills would be needed in rebuilding the Puget Sound city. Austin, although only 23 years old, already had many years of experience driving teams of horses. He quit school early in the ninth grade after being wrongfully expelled for vandalism. Austin chose to help his father haul wood instead of returning to school when the real culprit was identified.

A quick view of the smoldering ruins of Seattle's business district confirmed Lathrop's conviction that a strong body and good horses would be more useful than a high school education. He immediately wired his father to send him draft animals trained to haul Wisconsin lumber. When the teams arrived he already had lined up enough jobs hauling away debris to earn recognition as a "boy contractor." By the end of the year Seattle was well on the way to recovery and Austin was ready to accept a new challenge.

Young Lathrop directed his attention to an island 50 miles north of Seattle where land needed to be cleared for Anacortes, Washington, proclaimed to be the prime future port on Puget Sound. The April 1890 issue of *Pacific Magazine* described the new city in these glowing terms:

> Three months age the townsite of Anacortes was a

thick forest of spruce and cedar, scarcely a sign of which remains today, save, perhaps, the charred roots of some great tree which the fire has not entirely consumed. When the writer visited Anacortes — in the latter part of March (1890) — the town presented a curious sight. The trees had been recently cut down and removed to the saw-mills. Thousands of burning stumps sent forth great clouds of smoke that floated far over the straits. At night these fires were constantly watched and attended by hundreds of laborers. The landscape seemed a lake of fire, through which the dark figures of men were constantly moving, reminding one of the scenes in the Inferno ...

The streets are crowded with day laborers, who are employed on the railroad or in suburbs working the timber. Saloons are filled to overflowing. Gambling halls are in full blast...

Of course the 2500 restless indomitable people who came here two months ago when Anacortes was a forest with one store and a saloon, and identified themselves with this place, are prospecting all the embellishments of which cities are proud and without which they would not be deemed even towns. An electric railroad is busy in its preliminary work of seeking subsidies of land and making surveys before beginning the season's work of construction.

Lathrop secured contracts to clear streets in Anacortes and, subsequently, to build the electric railroad. Two brothers from Philadephia, named Potter, had sold eastern investors on the construction this railroad from Anacortes to Fidalgo City for distribution of the island farm corps to growing mainland markets. The prospects were so bright that Lathrop sent for his parents and two sisters to join him. He also made plans to marry 18-year-old Maude Woodcock, who was his special guest on the inaugural jaunt of the Anacortes Railroad in the spring of 1893.

After the railroad dedication, Lathrop leased 600 acres on Protection Island off the coast of Port Townsend where he built homes for himself and his family. The family compound also included docks, a hunting resort, and a model poultry farm.

Former President Benjamin Harrison, one of the guests at Protection Island, became Austin's friend and hunting companion and may have influenced him to be a life-long Republican. The poultry farm, with 5,000 laying hens, 2,500 chicks hatching every three weeks, and a new plan for date-stamping eggs for market, was progressing admirably when the Panic of '93 hit the Pacific Northwest. Young Lathrop hoped to pay for these developments with money he had earned in Anacortes, but the eastern investors declared bankruptcy and never made payment for the work he did on the railroad. Lathrop was forced to give up the buildings and projects on Protection Island and move his family to a small house in Seattle. With no work and debts to pay, Lathrop abandoned thoughts of marriage and even pawned the gold watch Maude had given him to get money for food.

TURNAGAIN ARM — 1896-1900
Captain of the *L.J. Perry*

Many unemployed men roamed the streets and docks of Seattle looking for opportunities to recover what they had lost in the Panic of '93. Frequently their eyes turned towards Alaska where occasional returning prospectors told of gold strikes. One day in the fall of 1895 Lathrop was in a waterfront saloon hoping for a free meal when he met a seafaring acquaintance named Kelly. Captain Kelly had just talked to some prospectors who told him of a new gold discovery on Cook Inlet in Alaska. The two men foresaw a demand for the transport of men and supplies to Alaska and considered obtaining a boat. Lathrop remembered the *L.J. Perry*, a 110-foot steam schooner that had transported hay for his horses while he was working in Anacortes. Although he had no money, Lathrop's credit was still good. He was able to persuade A.E. Barton, an associate in the Frye meat packing house, to advance him money to buy a half interest in the *L.J. Perry*. The other half interest was purchased by John O'Neil who planned to serve as chief engineer. Captain Kelly signed on as skipper and Lathrop, a midwesterner with no boating experience, agreed to be purser and business manager.

The three men put the small vessel into drydock at Ballard and spent the winter preparing it for rough going in sub-Arctic waters. On April 9, 1896, a year before news of the Klondike gold discovery reached Seattle, the *L.J. Perry* left Galbraith Dock with a cargo of supplies for the Alaska Commercial Company headquarters in Kodiak. The first voyage was an eventful one. While docked at Juneau, a mining camp on Gastineau Channel, they ran into unexpected business because 80 men headed for the Circle City gold strike were stranded there. The

Perry did not have the proper papers to haul these passengers to the base of the Chilkoot Trail at Dyea, but managed to find several small boats that were properly licensed. They were then able to load the men on the small boats and tow them to Dyea behind the *Perry*. Among these men were two who would become wealthy and famous in subsequent gold stampedes, Tex Rickard and T.J. Libby.

The sailing schooner *L.J. Perry* that Cap Lathrop used to transport miners on Turnagain Arm. *Photo courtesy of UAF.*

Before reaching their destination at Kodiak, the *Perry* picked up some other miners and took them to their prospects on Lituya Bay. While cruising in the waters around Yakutat they were twice approached by Natives trying to sell them wives. Lathrop gave one of the Indians some money but declined the offer of the woman. One of the prospectors, on the other hand, thus acquired his wife and is said to have lived happily ever after. While cruising along the Gulf of Alaska, a storm blew them close to shore at Katalla, where a prospector named Tom Smith rowed out to the *Perry* and told them about oil seepages in the area. At Kodiak they discharged the Alaska Commercial Company freight and loaded more for Cook Inlet.

At the coaling station on a sandspit in Kachemak Bay they encountered another group of stranded gold seekers. News of potential gold strikes in the Cook Inlet country had prompted several hundred men to come north on the *Lakme* and the

Utopia, but these larger vessels were held back by ice floes and the prospectors were forced to camp on the spit. Furthermore, Captain Johnny O'Brien of the *Utopia* had suffered an attack of acute appendicitis and was having an emergency operation performed by one of the prospectors in the galley of a stranded boat on the Homer spit. The *Perry* was able to continue on up Cook Inlet with some of the miners, while others built their own skiffs.

Lathrop and his associates were foresighted in their choice of a boat. The *Perry* was ideal for the Cook Inlet run since it had a shallow draft and could use either sail or steam power. The little ship burned coal which was mined locally from the beaches and cliffs of Kachemak Bay. Lathrop and his crew would paddle shallow scows to the beach at high tide and use crowbars to loosen chunks of coal exposed when the tide receded. Upon return to the *Perry* they shoveled coal directly into the furnace.

The crew of the *Perry* found that they could also obtain fresh meat at the old Russian village of Ninilchik on their first voyage up Cook Inlet. This village was a retirement community for Russians who had not returned to Russia after the purchase of Alaska by the United States. The *Perry* was the first vessel that the inhabitants had seen in 30 years. The climate had been good for the fair-skinned Russians, but their cattle were dwarfed as a result of inbreeding.

The major gold prospects in the Cook Inlet area were along the south side of Turnagain Arm at the small communities of Sunrise and Hope, and across the Arm at Girdwood and Bird Creek. Most of the miners working in this area before 1896 had anchored at Portage Bay on Prince William Sound and reached Turnagain Arm by crossing the Portage Glacier. Few ships ventured into Turnagain Arm because of the high tides. Della Banks, one of the early prospectors, described the Arm as she approached it on the tugboat *Canby*:

> The Arm is twenty-five miles long, narrow, and bordered by mountains It can be entered only at high tide, for at low tide it is nothing but mud flats. A bar at the entrance causes the water to pile up and go in in a large bore, sweeping everything before it. Woe betide the small

craft caught on the mud flats by the ebb tide, since the incoming flood tide will swamp her. ...

I was too excited to sleep. An hour later I went from the cabin to the deck to see what was going on. I was standing at the rail when the mate yelled suddenly, "Hold on there!" Came a creak and a groan, and the world seemed to slither out from under me. The *Canby* kneeled over on her side in a mud ravine, and hung there tilted at a forty-five degree angle.

Just the tide going out, that was all. Captain Durfee came through his window like a shot. Luckily, I happened to be on the upper side of the ship, else I'd have landed in the mud.[1]

The larger ships came up Cook Inlet as far as the Indian village of Tyonek, the site of an Alaska Commercial Company trading post and store. The *Perry* stopped regularly at Tyonek to pick up passengers and supplies for the prospectors on Turnagain Arm. The dock at Sunrise had two slips, one for the *Perry* and the other for smaller sailboats and rowboats belonging to the miners. Occasionally the *Perry* would also tow smaller boats up the Arm, as described by Della Banks:

We waited at Tyonik(sic) for the *Perry* to tow us to Sunrise, as Edmund didn't want to try sailing lest we by caught in the wind of Turnagain Arm. It was a rough trip. The waves dashed over the bow but our sloop didn't leak to amount to anything. We stayed with her, ready to cut loose if necessary. Passing Hope City on Resurrection Creek without stopping, we reached Sunrise on Six Mile Creek, twelve miles above, late in the evening.

The prospectors along the shores and creeks of Cook Inlet soon came to rely upon the *Perry* to bring them supplies, mail, and news of the outside world. Della Banks reports that many of the prospectors wondered why a rugged young man like Austin Lathrop was content to run a boat while there were riches in gold waiting to be found. They thought that he must be lazy and lacking in ambition, but Lathrop, through careful planning and fortuitous timing, soon controlled a lucrative monopoly. He enjoyed financial success and also frequently rescued penniless prospectors and helped them leave Alaska.

The *L.J. Perry* (left) at the Sunrise dock. *Photo courtesy of UAF.*

Lathrop returned to Seattle in the winter of 1896 with ample resources to marry, but found that Maude Woodcock had already married someone else. He did, however, persuade his father to come to Alaska with him the following year to build a cabin and start a trading post at Sunrise. Austin was not content to continue as purser on the *Perry*, so he got some books, locked himself in his room for a week to study, and passed the examination for his master's license. Captain Kelly continued to work with Lathrop on the *Perry* for part of 1897, but then got a job as pilot on another boat, the steamer *Clara Nevada* which blew up with all hands while coming down Lynn Canal.[2] Soon Lathrop, known as "Turnagain Arm Jim," bought out O'Neil, his other partner, and was owner, business manager, and captain of the *L.J. Perry* for the next four years.

When word of the Klondike gold strike reached Turnagain Arm in August 1897, many of the miners left the area. Lathrop, himself, brought this news to Sunrise, as reported by Della Banks:

I shall never forget that night! Captain Austin Lath-

rop stood on the steps of the store and told the growing crowd of the ship-load of gold from the Klondike - that 'ton of gold' which sent thousands stampeding into the little-know Yukon.
I'm going!' was the universal cry. The *Perry* and the *Stella Erland* left on the flood tide, and on them left men who had simply dropped everything and stepped aboard. Within twelve hours, Sunrise was practically depopulated.[3]

Lathrop was not one to drop everything and head to the Klondike. He continued to serve the prospectors who mined on Cook Inlet, and in the summer of 1898 had the opportunity to serve another type of client. In an effort to find an All-American route to the gold fields, the United States Army sent a party of men under the command of Captain E.F. Glenn into Cook Inlet to explore possible overland routes to the Yukon River. Capt. Glenn described their arrival in his official report:

We rounded Cape Elizabeth in the early morning of May 31, and consumed the remainder of the day and until nearly midnight in reaching Tyoonok(sic), at which place we found scattered along the beach from 200 to 500 prospectors, about 100 Indians (men, women, and children), and the trading station of the Alaska Commercial Company...

After examining this place I determined to place the command in camp at Ladds Station, located 5 miles farther up the inlet, about 2 miles above the North Foreland, and at the mouth of the Sushitna(sic) River. At this point we were entirely separated from and would not be brought into daily contact with the large number of miners, prospectors, and Indians then located at Tyoonok.

We used the *Perry* as a lighter. I finished my correspondence and discharged the cargo about the middle of the afternoon. By hard work of all hands until midnight we succeeded in pitching enough canvas to shelter the command.

The stock I caused to be brought up the beach at low tide, at which time the Sushitna River is easily forded at its mouth, where it breaks up into several small, shallow channels. At high tide this stream carries enough water to float steamers like the *Perry*, which is convenient for loading or unloading stock.

The *L.J. Perry* on the mud flats of Turnagain Arm while transporting horses for the Glenn Expedition in 1898. *Photo courtesy of UAA.*

Glenn wrote that the *Perry* was called upon again when he prepared to send Lieut. J.C. Castner and a party of men over to Knik Arm to cut a trail that could be used later to travel inland with horses and mules:

> Rations for this party for thirty days were packed and arrangements made with the *Perry* for transporting them across to the Knik Arm. In the afternoon this steamer anchored in the Sushitna River so as to load the stock. Shortly after this a heavy windstorm came up and prevented the party and freight from going on board for nearly three days.
>
> During this storm the tide raised to a much greater height than at any previous time, caught the steel boat belonging to the command and carried it out to sea, notwithstanding the fact that the boat itself was pulled farther up on shore than usual and was made fast by means of the painter with more than usual care...
>
> On June 6, at about half flood in the afternoon, the

stock, goods, etc. of the Castner party were taken on board, when we steamed to Tyoonok, and cast anchor to await the turn of the tide. While lying at anchor, and until we arrived opposite Fire Island the following morning, the vessel rolled and pitched so badly that our stock were constantly and violently thrown upon the deck.

We reached Knik Inlet finally, cast anchor, and waited for the vessel to go aground before attempting to unload. We were deeply impressed with the appearance of everything in this inlet. The weather was much more advanced than at Tyoonok or at Ladds Station by at least three weeks.

Later in the month Glenn arranged to purchase horses at Sunrise and needed the *Perry* to transport them for the exploring expedition up Knik Arm and the Matanuska River. This time Glenn described the difficulty of crossing Cook Inlet quicksand:

On the 17th day of July, knowing positively that I could secure the stock without delay, I loaded all necessary rations and men aboard the *Perry*, and about 10:30 p.m. sailed for Sunrise City, arriving the following morning. On that and the following day I secured 25 head of horses and mules, and by the evening of the 20th had loaded them on board and was ready to sail for Knik Station, where we arrived at daylight the following morning.

To avoid crossing a couple of boggy streams between the fishing village and the Knik Station, we induced the *Perry* to land just above the station, where, by going through a narrow channel, a good landing could be made and the stock could be brought ashore with safety and ease.

To avoid any possible danger in getting ashore at this point, where the waters were unknown to the pilot of the boat, I went up to the station, secured a pilot, and was just rowing out with him to meet the *Perry* when the pilot, either through a misunderstanding or some other cause unknown to us, and notwithstanding the fact that a flag had been placed on the sand bar to indicate the location of the channel, managed to run the bow of his boat onto the sand bar, whose banks were almost perpendicular at that point. He did not seem to realize or appreciate what he had done, as he continued to go ahead with full steam until the greater portion of the boat was hard aground on this bar, too hard, in fact, to shove or pull her off. Our situation was most critical. The tide had just commenced to ebb, and should we leave our stock and freight on board it was a foregone conclusion that the boat itself would be lost, as she was not strong enough to carry the weight on board of her when the tide ran out. It was necessary, therefore, to unload the stock at once. This meant a probable loss of all of them, as this bar was practically a mud bank, on which they would surely bog. Fortune seemed to favor us, however, on this point, for we found by spreading hay on the surface we could prevent their bogging at the point of landing. We were nearly half a mile from shore, however, with a channel intervening, to cross which we would have to swim the stock unless we waited until the water had completely run out. I decided upon the latter alternative, and tested the intervening space as much as possible in hopes I would find some place without quicksand, but without success. In sheer desperation I finally selected one horse that I would sacrifice if necessary, and started him across. Much to my surprise he reached the shore safely. We then tried to send across one at a time, but had succeeded on only starting a couple when the herd broke away from us and started pellmell for the shore, which they reached in safety. We learned then that the stock could be useful in soft ground, and subsequent experience corroborated this.

In the meantime some of our goods had been transferred from the *Perry* to a Columbia River boat. The remainder we were forced to carry by hand across the quicksand. The fate of the *Perry* hung in the balance until the tide came in, which, by good fortune, was somewhat higher than that of the morning, and high enough to float her, so that she escaped without serious injury.[4]

The *Perry* was on hand to transport the Glenn party when

they returned from the Interior in October. Glenn accompanied the little schooner on a trip to the "Coal Banks" about 12 miles north of Homer. He described how five men from the crew mined 60 tons during two tides and loaded it on the *Perry* to be transported to Sunrise City "to be used for general purposes by the inhabitants during the ensuing winter." The *Perry* remained in Cook Inlet waters transporting grain for the Army expedition until the end of October when it steamed down to Kuskatan to pick up a Geological Survey party under the charge of Mr. Spurr. Since the small schooner did not have sufficient power to make way against the winter winds it needed to be towed down the Inlet by a larger boat. On October 28, Glenn commented: "We got underway early in the morning, with the *Perry* still in tow. Shortly after starting we ran into a snowstorm which lasted at intervals throughout the day. About 11 a.m. we encountered quite a swell from the sea that sent all hands below. After this we cut loose from the *Perry*. She was rendered assistance by the *Dora* and not again seen by us."

VALDEZ AND COAL BAY — 1901-1908
Oil and Marriage Don't Mix

Captain A.E. Lathrop and the *L.J. Perry* continued to live a charmed life on the treacherous waters of Cook Inlet for the next two summers. In the winter, when ice clogged the Inlet, Lathrop returned to Seattle where he met Mrs. Lillian McDowell, an attractive widow with a 14-year-old daughter. Both mother and daughter cruised with him on Cook Inlet the next summer, and soon the Captain again began considering marriage.

Marriage, however, was not Lathrop's only new interest. While docked at Kodiak in 1900, Jack Lee, one of his crew, expressed a desire to go prospecting on the Alaska Peninsula, and Lathrop agreed to grubstake him. Lee returned with a small flask of oil and tales of bear with oil-matted fur and of Indians cleaning their guns with oil. Although prospecting for gold had never intrigued Lathrop, oil was another proposition. Both Lathrop and Lee filed claims for land at Coal Bay, on the Pacific side of the Alaska Peninsula near Lake Becharof. Oil seeps in this region had been known for years, but no serious drilling had been undertaken.

For once Lathrop's timing was not ideal. His two ambitions were not necessarily compatible. The marriage came first. On February 18, 1901, the first wedding in the history of Valdez took place at the residence of the Reverend D.W. Crane in which he united Captain Austin E. Lathrop and Mrs. Cosby McDowell. Captain O.A. Johnson of the *Bertha* was best man and Miss Cleo McDowell, daughter of the bride, was bridesmaid. The couple announced that they planned to make their home aboard the *L.J. Perry*.[5] On February 23, *The Alaskan* printed a short article stating that "Capt. Austin

21

Lathrop (Turnagain Arm Jim) will operate his popular little steamer *Perry* on Prince William Sound this summer instead of on the treacherous waters of Cook Inlet."

The newly-wed Lathrops and Miss Cleo soon became prominent in the social circles of Valdez, a three-year-old community where miners, prospectors, road-builders, and business people were beginning to settle with their families. In late August the trio were honored at a series of parties, one of which was described in the August 24 issue of the *The Valdez News*:

> On Thursday evening the Valdez Social Club gave a farewell social to Miss Cleo McDowell, who is to leave on the *Bertha* with her mother for several weeks visit to Seattle and other Sound cities. The large city hall was crowded with leading Valdez society people at 10 o'clock and twenty-four couples took part in the opening grand march. Dancing continued until midnight when an intermission was had and the ladies served a nice and appetizing lunch. Every number on the program was enjoyed and especially the Two Steps, Waltz Quadrille and Virginia Reel. During the wee small hours the Home Sweet Home waltz was danced and the guests departed for their homes, each and all saying that it was one of the most successful dances of the season.

The following week the Society column of the *The Valdez News* carried the following item:

> Capt. and Mrs. Austin Lathrop and Miss Cleo McDowell, daughter of Mrs. Lathrop, Judge L.L. Williams and Mr. Ed. C. VanBrundt were outgoing passengers on the *Bertha*. They were accompanied as far as Swanport by about twenty of their friends. The party had a very pleasant trip and bid many fond adieus to their departing friends. There was some kissing going on at the parting scene, but the reporter being a very bashful young man cannot say much regarding that part of the program. Captain and Mrs. Lathrop will make an extended trip to the eastern cities and visit the Pan-American Exposition. Miss McDowell

will visit friends in Seattle until their return. They will be greatly missed in society circles in Valdez and will be welcomed home when they return, which will be about the middle of October.

Lathrop also had business interests to attend to on his trip to the Pan American Exposition in Buffalo, where President William McKinley was assassinated early in September. He had not been successful in persuading westcoast financiers to back his oil exploration but heard that J.H. Costello, a wealthy Buffalo capitalist, might be interested in his project. The Lathrops did not return to Valdez in October, but the following spring *The Alaska Prospector* announced that "Capt. A. Lathrop was a passenger on the *Excelsior* on his way to Dry Bay in Cook Inlet with a large force of men and materials for opening up his oil property at that location."[6] Although Lathrop's sea-faring days were over, people continued to refer to him as "Captain Lathrop" and the nickname "Cap" stayed with him for the rest of his life. The *L.J. Perry* did not fare well under its new skippers. The small schooner sailed the waters of Prince William Sound, carrying pleasure excursions, until October 1903 when it was sold to J.W. Ivey and G.D. Corlew of Kayak.[7] The stormy waters around Katalla proved too much for the *Perry* which ran aground and sank on Kayak Island on October 23, 1904 because it did not have sufficient power to steam against the 60-80 Knot winds.[8]

When the Lathrop family returned to Valdez, *The Valdez News* announced on November 2, 1902: "Mrs. Austin Lathrope(sic) and daughter, Miss Cleo McDowell, were arrivals on the *Excelsior* from Seattle. Mrs. Lathrope and Miss McDowell are well known in Valdez, they having resided here nearly a year. Mr. Lathrope is now in Iliamna, but is expected here on the next boat. They will probably reside in Valdez during the winter." On December 20th *The Valdez News* carried the additional information that "the second floor of the building occupied by Brownell's Hardware store has been leased by Capt. and Mrs. Lathrope and will be fitted up as a first class lodging house." Items detailing the social activities of mother and daughter continued to appear in the papers during the winter, usually using the new spelling of the name.

In the meantime the Captain was busy making arrangements for activities on the Alaska Peninsula. On May 21, 1903 *The Valdez News* printed the following article:

> Active operations have commenced on the oil property at this place. The *Excelsior* which has just arrived here brought up Capt. Austin Lathrope, who made the first locations here and who has organized a rich company that will do extensive work here this summer. The *Excelsior* also brought up a large amount of freight, including ten head of horses, wagons, lumber, provisions and tools. The *Nome City* will bring 600 tons of freight on its next trip. This shipment will include drills, piping and machinery for seven wells, which will be put down this season. A hotel, store, warehouse, barns and dwellings will be erected at once. Sixty men will be employed by the company which Capt. Lathrope represents, and there are many other companies and individuals who will employ many men. It is expected that there will be between 300 and 500 people here by the middle of the summer.
>
> Capt. Lathrope has sold a large interest in his property here to J.H. Costello, a wealthy resident of Buffalo, N.Y., and there will be no lack of money to push the work at this place.
>
> No wells have yet been sunk but the oil bubbles up out of the ground in several places, and the indications are that there will be a heavy flow when the wells are down a short distance.

The next issue of *The Valdez News* lamented: "Mrs. Austin Lathrope and daughter Miss Cleo, will leave on the *Nome City* for Coal Bay where they will spend the summer with Capt. Lathrope, who is in charge of extensive oil operations at that place. They will be greatly missed in Valdez, especially in society circles."

Lathrop attempted to make a comfortable home for his wife and stepdaughter, but the small oil-boom settlement on the Alaska Peninsula did not suit the socially active teenager. Miss Cleo persuaded her mother to return to the Seattle area the next fall, and the ladies did not even go back again to the social circles of Valdez.[9] Lathrop was not having much luck in reaching oil either. The Costello money, an up-to-date derrick and Diamond drill, and an expert driller from the East were not sufficient to assure success during the summer of 1903. The first attempt was abandoned after a few hundred feet because of a crooked hole and the derrick moved to another site.[10] Another company drilling nearby on tracts staked by Jack Lee did encounter enough oil to keep hopes alive, but their well filled up with water.[11]

Lathrop returned to the Alaska Peninsula in 1904, the September 15 issue of *The Alaska Prospector* announcing that "A. Lathrop and J.H. Costello Jr. passed through here on their way to Coal Bay where they will put in the winter boring for oil in the interest of the Costello Oil Land Co." They planned to take about 40 men with them. Drilling had continued on the adjoining tracts throughout the summer. All of the groups working on the Alaska Peninsula that winter were able to keep warm by burning the oil- soaked peat mined from the local marshes.[12] Lathrop continued to drill near Lake Becharof throughout the summer of 1905 without success, and finally returned to Valdez in late August.[13]

Michael J. Heney's first work gang on the Copper River Railroad. *Photo courtesy of Anchorage Museum.*

Oil exploration in remote areas of Alaska was expensive business, and after 1905, financiers preferred to invest in the more readily available new discoveries in Texas and California. Capitalists were more interested in the recent copper discoveries in Alaska and intent upon constructing railroads to transport the copper to tidewater in Prince William Sound. Lathrop, still committed to a future in Alaska, returned to driving teams of horses. In the summer of 1906 he had a contract laying ties near the new town of Cordova for the Copper River Railroad, started by M.J. Heney, builder of the White Pass and Yukon. When Heney sold his fledgling railroad to the Guggenheim-Morgan interests in the fall of 1906, Lathrop gave up the contract at Sheep Bay and moved his teams back to Cordova.[14]

During the next winter Lathrop returned to California and succeeded in persuading financiers there to subsidize copper mining on Roaring Creek, a southern tributary of the Kotsina River where two of his Valdez friends, J.R. Gelineau and Joe Bell, had promising claims. He returned to Valdez in January 1907 with more horses, but encountered bad luck enroute. *The Valdez News,* on January 26, noted:

> Austin Lathrop lost one of the finest teams of horses ever shipped to Alaska. The team was brought from the east for the Seattle fire department but because they did not perfectly match they were sold to Mr. Lathrop. One of them died on the boat coming up and the other after he landed here. Like several other eastern horses shipped up lately they were affected with lung trouble. The team cost $650.

Not daunted by this loss, Lathrop continued with his plans for copper mining in the Kotsina district. On February 7, 1907, *The Alaska Prospector* described his progress:

> The outfit of the California-Alaska Mining & Development Co., in charge of J.R. Gelineau and Austin Lathrop, has moved camp to Wortman's and will soon have their freight over the summit. This company is a close corporation organized by California parties to develop the

properties known as the Native Copper group, located by Gelineau and Bell last summer on the Kotsina.

They will spend from $25,000 to $40,000 on the development of the property this summer. The claims adjoin the ground on which The Great Northern Development Co. has a bond.

Joe Bell is expected on the next boat and will join Gelineau and Lathrop. Their outfit consists of about 40 tons of freight and 12 men are in their employ.

The work in the summer of 1907 was largely confined to doing assessment work because of the large number of claims held by the company and the distance of the claims from the source of supply. However *The Katalla Herald* reported on August 31, 1907 that the company had first-class copper showing with an 800-pound copper nugget taken out of one of the ledges.

Cordova street scene in 1908. *Photo courtesy of Anchorage Museum.*

The 1907 United States Geological Survey Bulletin mentions tunnels dug by the California-Alaska Mining and Development Company, but most of the excitement in copper mining centered around the rich Bonanza discovery near the Kennicott Glacier.

Severe winter storms in the fall of 1907 washed out a breakwater at Katalla, and the Guggenheim-Morgan Alaska Syndicate decided to use Cordova as the port city for the railroad they were building to the Bonanza copper mine. Upon return from the Kotsina, Lathrop realized that there would be plenty of work for his teams building the new city of Cordova. This time his timing was good. In partnership with a man named Keys, Lathrop organized the Alaska Transfer Company. By December of 1908 he had bought out his partner.[15]

In the early days of the Alaska Transfer Company, Captain Lathrop established a good reputation by hauling lumber, coal, and anything else that people needed to have transported. He often shoveled and loaded the coal himself. Among other jobs, Lathrop and the new Presbyterian minister and artist, Eustace Ziegler, were responsible for carrying corpses to the local cemetery. Years later, when Ziegler gave up the ministry and became one of Alaska's leading artists, he gave Lathrop a painting showing the two men enroute to the cemetary.[16] The Alaska Transfer Company met all of the ships that docked at Cordova. An editorial in the February 6, 1909 issue of the *Cordova Daily Alaskan* described a dilemma facing the local chamber of commerce:

> The chamber of commerce held an interesting session last evening. The matter of having a free bus to and from all steamers was considered. For some time Capt. Lathrop has been giving everybody a free ride to and from all steamers at his own expense but "horse feed" costs money. The people who climb into Capt. Lathrop's sleighs without invitation are like unto the man who would go into your place of business and help himself to your groceries, your whiskey, your cigars, the victuals on your table or anything else, for taking people to and from the steamers is Capt. Lathrop's way of making money. There are some people in Cordova who would run a willing horse to death. The chamber is willing to pay Capt. Lathrop for the transportation of passengers from the steamers who may wish to visit town, but not to give a free ride to those of the town, who, as a rule, would not even give five cents to the chamber of commerce. The chamber of commerce can not afford it, neither can we understand how Capt. Lathrop does.

With the expansion of his draying business in Cordova, Lathrop was starting a new era in his life. The February 12, 1910 issue of the *Cordova Daily Alaskan* carried the following article:

> Capt. Austin Lathrop today received a telegram conveying the sad news of the death of has wife yesterday in Seattle. Deceased was 39 years of age and has been an invalid for the past two years. Besides her husband she leaves a married daughter, Mrs. J.A. Boyce. The funeral will take place in Seattle tomorrow.
>
> Mrs. Lathrop spent more than a year at Valdez during which time she made many friends and was greatly loved for her womanly traits. The sympathy of the community is extended to Capt. Lathrop.

That same year conservation interests succeeded in closing the Alaska Peninsula to further oil drilling. Austin Lathrop was 45 years old and had watched several fortunes come and go. The two projects, marriage and drilling for oil, to which he had devoted the past ten years, had not been successful, but his prospects in Cordova looked good.

CORDOVA — 1909-1914
A New City to Build

As soon as he established his transfer business in Cordova, Captain Lathrop began to earn a reputation for providing exemplary service. On April 27, 1909, the *Cordova Daily Alaskan* ran a short article stating:

> Capt. Lathrop is manager of the Alaska Transfer Co., and though only having been in Cordova since last fall, he has a number of fine teams, and is doing a large percentage of the transportation business in the city. He has a number of vehicles, substantial and light rigs, ordered for the summer trade, and his outfit will compare favorably with many city firms. His stables are centrally located under the Arctic Lumber Co.'s building on C avenue, and are provided with every facility for serving the public with promptness and dispatch.

The financial reverses of the past 20 years, however, taught Lathrop not to commit all resources to one enterprise. As soon as he accumulated enough money, he began to diversify his interests. Early in 1910 he bought out the Arctic Lumber Company, thus taking over its ice house and gaining control over the "frozen fluid" business.

In addition to providing good service, Lathrop always looked ahead and made sure that he had the most up-to-date equipment. On a trip to San Francisco in January 1910, he arranged for the delivery of "one of the latest model touring automobiles." *The Cordova Daily Alaskan* announced the upcoming purchase on January 13:

For some time the captain has been figuring on this innovation and he considers that the time has arrived when a car will not only prove a paying investment, but also a great convenience to the traveling public.

It will be a forty-horse power machine and will comfortably seat seven people. All boats and trains will be met with the auto, which will also be at the service of those desiring it for pleasure purposes. By the proper advertising on the different vessels that stop here from Seattle, as well as from the westward, a large number of people who are passing through will take the advantage of the opportunity to 'See Cordova' when they can do so in a buzz wagon.

The *Alaskan* would suggest that when the captain is in San Francisco and Seattle that he have a streamer painted with appropriate lettering, attach it to the auto and let the people out in the states know that the metropolis of Alaska is thoroughly up-to-date.

The wonderful White steamer arrived in Cordova on March 21, and the newspaper commented that "this machine is a great climber and can be used on any street in the city." The new automobile was a special attraction at local celebrations. After school children put on a musical program for Flag Day in 1910, Captain Lathrop treated them to a ride around town.[17]

Cordova's first automobile with Captain Lathrop driving. *Photo Courtesy of Cordova Historical Society.*

Although *Alaska Yukon Magazine* did not list Lathrop as one of the leading business men in the 1910 Cordova issue, he was fast becoming a popular man with the reputation for being a practical joker.[18] Community activities relied on Lathrop for donations. His favorite charity was the local baseball team, as noted in the May 10, 1910 newspaper:

> The committee soliciting subscriptions for the baseball team and grounds are meeting with great success. Captain A. Lathrop was among the first to be approached in the matter and grasping a pen wrote a check for $200. Handing it over to the committee he smiled as they expressed their appreciation of the donation.

As a by-product of financial success and new-found popularity, Lathrop was lured into seeking elective office, although he had previously vowed never to go in to politics.[19] Lathrop was elected to be a delegate to the Alaska Republican Convention in June 1910, and, in March 1911, agreed to run for city council. Since he received the greatest number of votes, Lathrop was declared to be the mayor of Cordova. The editor of the *Cordova Daily Alaskan* commented: "Out of the full vote cast, Capt. A.E. Lathrop received all but 26, which was a fine tribute to his popularity and many exceptional

Cordova Coal Party —May 4, 1911. *Photo Courtesy of Alaska State Library.*

good qualities." Lathrop continued to participate actively in all of his enterprises. He was frequently observed in back yards shoveling coal from his trucks, and when the council announced the spring cleanup, Mayor Lathrop personally hosed down the sidewalks. Accounts vary as to how actively he may have participated in the Cordova Coal Party, the most noteworthy event of his term as mayor.

The Copper River and Northwestern Railroad was completed in April 1911 and copper ore was finally being brought from the Kennecott Mine to the port of Cordova. Cordova's prosperity, however, was hampered because the federal government had closed the nearby Bering River coal fields. The railroad and all other local businesses were, therefore, forced to buy expensive coal shipped in from British Columbia. Remembering the Boston Tea Party, the citizens of Cordova devised a scheme for publicizing their plight. For months they collected shovels and stored them behind Lathrop's Alaska Transfer Company warehouse.[20] On Thursday May 4, 1911, the *Cordova Daily Alaskan* printed the details under the front page banner headline CORDOVA HAS BOSTON TEA PARTY:

> Having lost patience at the dilatory tactics of the government in allowing the coal claims of bona fide entrymen to be opened up, a large force of men this afternoon gave Cordova a repetition of the famous Boston tea party by marching to the dock and, armed with shovels, proceeded to shovel the pile of foreign coal stored there into the bay. While there was considerable feeling among some of the participants in the affair, the crowd was an orderly but determined one and evidently meant business.
>
> As soon as Agent Barry realized what was about to happen he telephoned the marshal's office, but as Deputy Brightwell was down the bay on an important case, he was unable to get federal protection. Mayor Lathrop was then appealed to, but he was helpless to render the necessary assistance and he passed it up to the United States Commissioner. ... The United States Commissioner swore Mayor Lathrop and Chief of Police Dooley in as deputy marshals and, armed with warrants for the arrest

of the men causing the trouble, they immediately started for the dock. ...

Some of the crowd was willing to disperse, not wanting to question the authority of the deputized officers, but others insisted in going ahead, and soon all were again busy shoveling coal. The mayor, seeing that it was useless to further argue with the crowd, hurried uptown and sent a cablegram to Governor Clark appraising him of the condition of affairs. Late this afternoon the crowd was still in charge of the dock.

As news of the Cordova Coal Party hit nationwide newspapers, Mayor Lathrop quietly left town. Some people claim that he was the primary organizer of the protest.[21]

The following year Lathrop positively declined the honor of serving again as mayor[22], but continued to be elected to the city council until 1914 when the *Cordova Daily Alaskan* succeeded in persuading voters that the town was being run by too small a clique of business men. Lathrop's enterprises were so extensive that a visiting editor from Chicago observed that, after the local barber closed his shop, "Cap Lathrop locked up the rest of the town and threw away the key."[23]

Although Lathrop went back to survey the Kotsina copper claims in the summer of 1911, his main activities were in the town of Cordova. As local representative of the Olympia Brewing Company, he persuaded the company president Leopold Schmidt to spend the summer in Cordova personally superintending the building of a $60,000 concrete warehouse. The following year, the city council accepted Lathrop's offer to use part of the building as a city jail.[24]

Lathrop also served as local agent for the Alaska Coast Company and later for the Pacific Alaska Navigation Company. He helped organize a fish saltery in 1912, and, in 1914, became one of the initial directors of First Bank of Cordova. He continued to be active in the transfer business, erecting coal bunkers so that coal could be carried directly by chutes from incoming boats. In order to keep on meeting incoming Cordova visitors in style, he purchased the prize maroon White Big Six touring car at the Portland automobile show for about $5,500.[25]

While expanding his business activities, Lathrop continued to be active in community affairs. He helped organize the new Cordova Chamber of Commerce in 1913, donating use of half the office of the Alaska Transfer Company free of charge for two months. His new secretary, Miss Ruby DeGraff volunteered to do all necessary stenographic work.[26] Lathrop's other main community activity was the local baseball team and he worked hard to develop a ball park on the outskirts of town.

Plans for the ball park were temporarily suspended in June 1913 when seven local liquor dealers refused to contribute to the cause if the team went to Valdez for games over the 4th of July, thus depleting their holiday business in Cordova.[27] The team did go, splitting games with the Valdez team, and the ball field was eventually completed due to the contributions of Lathrop and other Cordova businessmen.

The Captain's community contributions were not limited to the Chamber of Commerce and the ball team. In April 1914 he contributed a "beautiful new morocco edition of the Messages and Papers of the Presidents" to the school library and *The Alaska Times* commented: "The action of Captain Lathrop should serve as an example to the other public spirited men of the town".

Captain Lathrop in Cordova about 1917. *Photo courtesy of Cordova Historical Society.*

In addition to making charitable contributions for community activities, Lathrop found a way to profit financially from entertaining his fellow Cordovans. On October 4, 1911, the *Cordova Daily Alaskan* announced:

> E.L. Harwood and A.E. Lathrop have taken a lease on the Donahoe building next to Clayson's clothing store. It is their intention to fix up the main part of the ground floor for a theatre, the furnishings for which will be purchased by Capt. Lathrop, who goes to the states on the *Sampson*. The floor is to be elevated and

Cordova Empress Theatre. *Photo courtesy of Alaska State Library.*

> a large stage erected. Three hundred and fifty opera chairs will be ordered and the theatre equipped with all modern conveniences. The lobby and entrance to the show house will be through the present barber shop and two stores will be fitted up in front of the

theatre. The second story will be rented for living and housekeeping purposes.

The new theater opened on November 18 with an admission charge of 25 cents and a program which included local singers and dancers and a drama entitled "Sailor Jack's Reformation." Within two years Lathrop bought out his partner and took over the management of the theater himself. Motion pictures were becoming popular and soon replaced local talent on the program. Lathrop, who rarely sat through an entire movie, imported the best recent productions to show at his Empress Theatre. He continued to feature some local talent as well, with the seven-piece Cordova Orchestra, consisting of violins, trombone, cornet, clarinet, drums and piano, presenting a special program on January 4, 1914. Lathrop also imported talent to perform at the Empress. In January 1914 the newspaper

Community gathering in Cordova's "Grand Theatre" about 1911. Lathrop in audience on left. *Photo courtesy of Mrs. Albert Swalling.*

mentioned that Captain A.E. Lathrop would return from Seattle "accompanied by a lady violinist for the Empress theater orchestra." Other young ladies contacted him, hoping to subsidize their trips to Alaska by performing at the Empress.[28]

Lathrop earned a reputation for entertaining visiting ladies when Editor James Keeley of the *Chicago Tribune* arranged to have him take care of a group of *Tribune* employees. *The Alaska Times* commented on July 13, 1913;

> There is nothing that should receive quicker response than a call for volunteers, a fellow townsman is in need of help. On the arrival of the *Alameda* yesterday morning Captain Lathrop was called upon to care for and entertain a bevy of beautiful young ladies consigned to him by his friend Editor James Keeley, of the *Chicago Tribune*. On the impulse of the moment the gallant Captain some time ago undertook to chaperon and entertain the young ladies while in Cordova. It is up to him now to make good. The Captain has for a number of years attempted to monopolize the attention of most of the fair sex travelling to Alaska, and while we cannot fail to envy him the present commission, we fear that Brother Keeley went a little too far, for every man has his limitations, and four handsome and accomplished young ladies is too much for even the gallant Captain. As we go to press the volunteer committee consists of about all the eligible young men in Cordova.

The next day the newspaper reported that the Captain had "exerted himself to the utmost" to make sure that the ladies had a good time, with a fishing trip and a show at the Empress.

The Empress Theatre became the center of social life in Cordova. Lathrop donated use of the theatre for political speeches, benefits for the baseball team, and even cancelled usual Sunday night shows for special religious functions.[29] Although he arranged for extensive remodeling of the theater in the summer of 1913, Lathrop began considering expansion into other Alaska cities.

When Lathrop settled in Cordova in 1908, he undoubtedly felt sure that the new Prince William Sound seaport would be the terminus of a railroad to the interior of Alaska and the population center of Southcentral Alaska. By 1914 he perceived that Cordova's future was less secure. The Alaska Syndicate, which built the Copper River and Northwestern Railroad, announced that it would not extend the railroad beyond the Kennecott mines unless the Bering River coal fields were opened for development. In the meantime the federal government authorized construction of the Alaska Railroad from tidewater to Fairbanks, but President Woodrow Wilson had not as yet decided whether the government railroad would utilize the Copper River or the Susitna Valley route. Lathrop spent the winter in Seattle, and on March 26, 1915, the *Cordova Daily Alaskan* printed a news release from Seattle which stated that Capt. A.E. Lathrop was remaining in Seattle for business reasons and "does not wish to depart for the north until after a definite announcement is made as to the ocean terminus of the government railroad." When President Wilson announced that the railroad would follow the Susitna rather than the Copper River Valley, Lathrop was ready. On May 14, 1915, the Cordova paper reported that "Capt. Lathrop had sent some teams and wagons to do drayage business" and "lumber to put up a building and establish a moving picture house at the new railroad construction camp on Ship Creek."

ANCHORAGE — 1915-1921
Movie Magnate of the Empress Theatres

Captain Lathrop was already an old hand at building new towns when he arrived at the tent city on the Ship Creek mud flats early in the summer of 1915. He no longer needed to depend on contracts and loans as he did 25 years before when he cleared land for Anacortes, Washington. Now he had a plan and sufficient money to construct the buildings he needed. The June 26 issue of the *Cook Inlet Pioneer* announced that, as soon as the new townsite for Anchorage was open, Captain Austin Lathrop would erect "one of the swellest theatres in the northland." Lathrop always preferred the British spelling, "theatre".

Lathrop Building in Anchorage. *Photo courtesy of Anchorage Museum.*

Lathrop had other building plans as well. Although he did not personally purchase lots at the land auction on July 10, he quickly acquired a choice lot at the corner of Fourth Avenue and H Street. On August 14, the newspaper reported that he had the "distinction of erecting the most commodious building in the new town" with "five fine roomy store spaces, already leased for various businesses". According to the paper, the building was substantially made, with the "best floor ever placed in an Alaska building." The frame Lathrop Building was soon open for business, but erecting Anchorage's first concrete structure to house the Empress Theatre required an additional year.

While planning for the Anchorage theater, Lathrop moved ahead with his plan to establish a chain of Empress theaters. On October 14, 1915, he arrived in Seward to open his 300-seat theater in the new Arctic Brotherhood hall with a showing of *The Sea Wolf*.[30] Lathrop spent a busy two weeks traveling between Seward, Cordova and Valdez. On October 28, the *Valdez Daily Prospector* ran the following article:

> The Empress theatre of Valdez will open its doors to the public tomorrow night and it truthfully can be said that Valdez now has the finest theatre in Alaska. It is owned by Capt. A.E. Lathrop, who owns a chain of Empress theatres in Cordova, Valdez, Seward, and will build at Anchorage as soon as electricity is available.
>
> The Empress theatre occupies the Blackwell building on McKinley Street which was specially designed and built for Capt. Lathrop by Chas. R. Crawford, the contractor. Everything in the building is new and modern, including a new full upright grand piano.
>
> The theatre has a seating capacity of three hundred on the main floor and a large box for parties will comfortably seat a dozen persons. The house is equipped with patent folding opera chairs, the kind that are used in all large amusement houses in the States.
>
> The operating room, located over the ticket office, is equipped with the latest machines and is absolutely fireproof. The new machines are so arranged that films cannot burn more than one inch even when set on fire. The room is lined with quarter-inch sheets of asbestos covered with heavy sheet steel. The openings from the room are so fitted that should fire break out in the room the audience would not be aware of the accident, as every

vent would automatically close and an iron asbestos lined airshaft open to carry off the fumes. ...

Particular attention has been paid to the decorations which are all hand work. The decorating has been done by H. Conklin of the firm of Conklin & Fitzgerald, who make a specialty of theatre work. A beautiful arch with silk lined plush curtains adds a finishing touch and a pleasing and harmonious effect. The picture curtain is of the latest Minusa gold fibre screen and is said to do away with the shimmery, flickering effect so often seen in moving pictures. ...

The Empress will open with the feature film, *An American Citizen* produced by the Famous Players company, with John Barrymore in the leading role. It is a comedy drama of high class which Capt. Lathrop ordered specially for the opening night and Manager Pinkus promises appropriate music by the Empress trio with all the pictures.

The Valdez claim to the finest theater in Alaska was short lived. On July 3, 1916, the Empress Theatre in Anchorage opened with the showing of a feature film starring Billie

Anchorage Fourth Avenue in 1917, showing Empress Theatre. *Photo courtesy of Anchorage Museum.*

Burke. Two days later the *Anchorage Daily Times* described part of the ceremony:

... Long, loud and continued calls for Captain Lathrop followed. The captain appeared and the applause that greeted him was of that deafening character that follows the prison scene in 'Il Trovatore' in which Caruso and Farrar are the principals. Bowing his acknowledgments, the captain said, 'I thank you from the bottom of my heart.' But these few words spoke volumes. Then the show was on.

Lathrop spent most of the rest of the summer in Seattle arranging for films to show at his theaters. On September 8, the *Anchorage Daily Times* announced that he had negotiated a contract with "the efficient Triangle Film corporation service, which deals strictly in clean, high-class dramas, comedies and various productions meeting with the demand of the moving picture public." The Empress circuit was reported to include Juneau, Ketchikan, Fairbanks and Nome in addition to Anchorage, Cordova, Valdez and Seward, but the paper was quick to specify that "naturally the most pretentious and beautiful is located in Anchorage."

While in Seattle, Lathrop met Charles Evans Hughes, the Republican presidential candidate, and strongly endorsed him. Although they belonged to different factions of the Republican party, Lathrop placed the Empress Theatre at the disposal of Delegate James Wickersham during his campaign tour of Anchorage.[31] The Empress Theatre catered to other groups as well, with front row seats reserved for Boy Scouts and other children on Saturday nights. The newspaper commented:

> While the time was long ago Captain Lathrop well remembers his youthful days when there were no moving picture houses to entertain and forms of amusement were entirely different. Today the genial Captain welcomes the boys to the theatre and naturally expects them to applaud and laugh for the Captain realizes that applause and laughter are contagious and inspiring to the organist, the audience, the ushers, and even the mute screen."[32]

Organ music became an integral theatre offering in 1917

when Lathrop installed a new Kimball Unit Orchestra pipe organ, taking "the place of a sixteen-piece orchestra and measuring 16 feet high and 28 feet long."[33] The installation of the organ prompted the *Anchorage Daily Times* to commend Lathrop in an editorial on June 27, 1917:

> Easily ranked among our foremost citizens in point of courage, faith, business ability and foresight, is Captain Austen(sic) E. Lathrop. Captain Lathrop is a man who does things. When he does things, he believes in doing them right. Money seems to be of secondary consideration with him. He has erected in this town the finest motion picture house in Alaska, a structure that would adorn and be a credit to an advanced and up-to-date city in the states. He made this heavy investment in this town when

Interior of Anchorage Empress Theatre. *Photo courtesy of Anchorage Museum.*

> its future was not assured, as now. The faith displayed by him at the time he erected this fine concrete building led others to make substantial improvements. His motion picture house ready for use, he made arrangements for the best motion pictures films that could be obtained. The reels displaying the Pathe-Hearst world news come direct from the factory to the Empress theatre in Anchorage.

He has just installed a Kimball Symphony Unit Organ, manufactured expressly for his theatre in Anchorage by the manufacturers in Chicago."

Interior of Anchorage Empress Theatre. *Photo courtesy of Anchorage Museum.*

Lathrop diversified his enterprises in Anchorage much as he had done in Cordova. In addition to the transfer company and the theater, he added a second floor to the Lathrop building to be used as apartments and a hotel. On April 24, 1917 the *Anchorage Daily Times* commented:

> Captain A.E. Lathrop is still building apartments and this time he has remodeled the space formerly used by the Transfer company into a modern place to be occupied by modern and moral young men, prominent in the social and business life of the city. The new ground floor apartments are modeled after college frat houses and will consist of a reception room, den, bed rooms, baths, etc. There will be no newel posts or circular stairways to contend with; there will be no cuckoo clocks to answer and everything will be absolutely stag.

Lathrop also was one of the original directors of the Bank of Anchorage,[34] which eventually merged with the National Bank of Alaska,[35] and served as a director of the Anchorage-Willow Creek Mining and Development Company.[36]

His popularity in the new railroad town, however, was enhanced by contributions that did not bring direct financial rewards, such as subsidizing a building for the Alaska Labor Union, as reported on December 22, 1916:

It was largely through the efforts of Captain A.E. Lathrop that the Alaska Labor Union was able to build their

Bank of Anchorage in the Empress Theatre building. *Photo courtesy of Anchorage Museum.*

magnificent edifice on the solid foundation of a prominent 4th avenue lot; in other ways he has helped the order in both finance and wisdom; always from the spirit of generosity and public spiritedness.

The committee in charge of the opening dance tomorrow night is merely a voice of the 3,000 members of the Alaska Labor Union who rose as one man and voted aye in the selection of Captain Lathrop to lead the grand march.

The selection is proper recognition of the captain's efforts in their behalf and moreover expresses their appreciation and gratitude.

The paper went on in a lighter vein to claim that Lathrop, who rarely participated in social events, was "a past master in the art of leading grand marches" and that "several intricate figures" had been named after him.

In spite of his popularity in Anchorage, Lathrop still had roots in Cordova and announced to the *Anchorage Daily Times* on January 30, 1917 that he was leaving W.G. Stoeser in charge of his extensive business in Anchorage and returning to Cordova to build an 800-seat concrete theater that would be "second only to the one in Anchorage." Lathrop took an active part in the construction in Cordova. On August 30, 1918 *The Cordova Daily Times* reported that Captain A.E. Lathrop met with a painful accident while superintending work on his new Empress theater building. He was struck on the head by a piece of falling lumber, receiving a severe gash that necessitated four stitches.

The Cordova theater was completed in 1918 under the direction of the architect George B. Purvis, and even the Anchorage paper admitted that the three and five story reinforced concrete building would be the "finest in all Alaska." Special features of the Cordova theater included a sidewalk of glass in a steel frame, resting on a concrete base,[37] and a large painting of Mt. McKinley by Sidney Lawrence.[38]

With similar enterprises in both Anchorage and Cordova, Lathrop was continually traveling between the two cities, with stops in Seward and Valdez to check up on the theaters there, and trips to Seattle to arrange for films. He relied heavily on Ruby DeGraff, who had been his personal secretary since 1910, to assist in supervising his enterprises. On October 10, 1918, *The Cordova Times* quoted an article from the *Anchorage Democrat* which provided insight into the rivalry between the two railroad towns in addition to describing the peripatetic lives of Miss DeGraff and her employer:

> Miss Ruby DeGraff is of the firm opinion that she is the most traveled lady in Anchorage, if not in Alaska. …
>
> In her efficient capacity as private secretary and mental advisor to Capt. A.E. Lathrop, the bloated movie magnate and landed proprietor, Miss DeGraff's duties necessitate many visits of a business nature to the different towns included in the Empress theater circuit. Of all these towns Anchorage is the favorite, and incidentally the best from

the standpoint of theater attendance. ... The people of Anchorage are always glad to hear of Cordova's business prosperity as substantiated by Miss DeGraff, and they also realize that the abundant rainfall is merely necessary to check the exuberance of elation caused by the unprecedented fishing, mining and general activity. ...

Miss DeGraff expects to again return to Cordova on the *Admiral Schley* and Captain Lathrop will go to Seattle to arrange for Anchorage's supply of winter photo-screen productions. According to present plans Captain Lathrop will visit Anchorage in about thirty days to be sworn in as a member of the advisory board, subscribe to the Republican campaign, donate to the Red Cross, and meet his many friends who are always glad to welcome his return.

On one of his business trips to Anchorage early in 1920, a delegation of citizens persuaded Lathrop to file as a Republican candidate for the territorial legislature.[39] He was enthusiastically endorsed in both Anchorage and Cordova and easily elected as representative from the third division.[40] When the legislature convened in Juneau in March 1921, Lathrop served on the following committees: Banks, Banking and Corporations; Fisheries, Fish, Game and Agriculture; Municipal Affairs; Transportation, Commerce and Navigation; and Ways and Means.[41] The session was generally reported to be non-productive, but on April 14, 1921, Senator Richard Elsner from Cordova created an uproar by introducing a memorial to Congress calling for self-government for Alaska with the election of two senators, a governor, a secretary and two representatives. The *Anchorage Daily Times* reported the next day that the memorial was defeated by a vote of nine to seven, but that Lathrop had voted in the affirmative. The legislative session finally adjourned in mid-May, as reported in the *Anchorage Daily Times*:

> Back from the arduous thankless duties as an Alaskan solon representing the third division Captain A.E. Lathrop, of Empress fame, arrived in Anchorage last night. The captain was fortunate in securing accommodations on the freighter *Latouche*, otherwise he would still be in

Juneau cussing his friends who practically railroaded him into office. Like Poe's raven Captain Lathrop says 'never again'; this goes for several things, but he emphasizes the fact that as a lawmaker he prefers the pick and shovel. But at that Captain Lathrop did yeoman service and upheld the dignity and rights of his constituents in an especially commendable manner."[42]

Although he retired from elective office, Lathrop remained active in the Republican party and dedicated to the development of Alaska's resources. He still believed that oil development would be profitable, investing in the Alaskatalla Petroleum Company with holdings in the Katalla area.[43] In an attempt to find oil in the Anchorage area, he helped raise funds to drill a well three miles from downtown Anchorage.[44] The July 9, 1921 issue of the *Cordova Daily Times* reported that "Capt. A.E. Lathrop is offering $100 to anyone who finds oil seepage within ten miles of the city of Anchorage."

Attempts to find oil near Anchorage failed, but with a new Republican administration in Washington, Lathrop anticipated that Alaska coal and oil fields would soon be opened for development. After a hiatus in construction during World War I, the Alaska Railroad was nearing completion and Lathrop anticipated opportunities for development in Fairbanks and along the Anchorage to Fairbanks railbelt.

THE CHEECHAKOS — 1922-1924
Alaska's Home-Grown Motion Picture

As the Alaska Railroad neared completion in 1922, Cap Lathrop prepared to expand his enterprises in interior Alaska. On February 3 the *Anchorage Daily Times* announced that he had obtained an interest in a Fairbanks theater and bought out the other partners. He had built a 500-seat theater two years previously at Nenana, the northern hub for railroad construction, but it was damaged by fire on March 25.[45] Although he was also preparing to take advantage of new federal policies that would enable development of oil wells on the Alaska Peninsula and coal mines near Nenana, for a year he devoted much of his money and energy to a new activity — the production of a moving picture in Alaska.

For several years motion pictures about Alaska, based on books by Jack London and Rex Beach, had thrilled audiences, but they were all filmed in other locations. A group of promoters from American Lifograph Company of Portland, Oregon, headed by George Edward Lewis, toured Alaskan towns in the summer of 1922 with a plan to produce a travelogue and feature film in Alaska. Alaskan businessmen welcomed this opportunity to publicize the territory and organized fund-raising committees in Seward, Anchorage, Fairbanks, Nenana and Cordova. The *Cordova Daily Times* mentioned on July 10 that the Anchorage Chamber of Commerce committee, headed by A.E. Lathrop and A.B. McDonald expected to raise $20,000. Later that month the same paper announced the formation of the Alaska Motion Picture Corporation with George Lewis as president and Lathrop as vice-president.[46] When the new corporation met in August, Captain A.E. Lathrop was unanimously elected president of the strictly Alaska company, which planned to produce a 12-reel picture, with three reels filmed in the participating towns followed by a nine-reel drama. To accomplish this, $75,000 was to be raised in Alaska by selling shares at $10 each, with an equal amount provided by the American Lifograph company by furnishing motion picture machinery and equipment.[47]

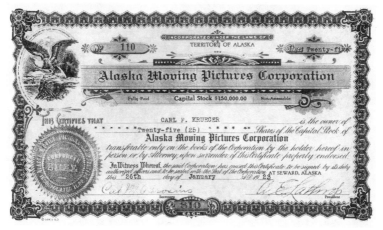

The *Cordova Daily Times* optimistically prophesied on July 31 that the stock might return twenty dollars for each dollar invested.

The stock sold quickly and, on November 13, 1922, construction started on a 7,000 square foot moving picture studio in downtown Anchorage. Lathrop, as president and general manager, was in charge of all work in Alaska while Lewis and L.H. Moomaw, the director, were choosing the stars and supporting actors. Anchorage looked forward to being the Hollywood of the North and the *Anchorage Daily Times* carried frequent updates on the building progress, including the installation of three floors of dressing rooms, complete darkroom facilities, and a movable platform 25 feet high for shooting scenes.

On March 8, 1923, the Anchorage paper announced that the entire cast of artists, recruited in Portland, New York and Hollywood, were enroute to Alaska. Lathrop and McDonald took the train to Seward to meet the arriving stars on March 14, and the next day approximately a thousand Anchoragites greeted the cast with a "free dance and jollification at the moviedrome." Taking advantage of the opportunity, Director Moomaw mounted the platform and directed the filming of several hundred couples dancing.[48]

Dance Hall scene in *The Cheechakos*. *Photo courtesy of Anchorage Museum.*

After a short rest, the cast and production crew boarded the Alaska Railroad for Mt. McKinley National Park where they filmed winter scenes with real dog teams to accompany the drama depicting gold-rush days. While the rest of the cast was filming these scenes, the Alaska Moving Picture corporation proudly announced the signing of a four-year-old child star, Miss Marguerite Schechert.[49]

The moving picture crew next took a private train to Girdwood, the small mining town on Turnagain Arm chosen to represent Skagway, where they planned to erect hundreds of tents and film night scenes with one hundred rockets "lighting the country for miles around." The *Anchorage Daily Times* provided the following description on April 4, 1923:

> Six moving picture cameras will be swung into use to catch every phase of the gigantic repetition of the days

of `97 and `98 showing a thousand camp fires, glowing softly through the night at the base of a lofty mountain pass, while impatient chechacoes (sic.) and grizzled, be-whiskered sourdoughs strut around the town anxiously waiting the break of dawn, signaling the rush of gold-seekers over the towering pass.

Private car on the Alaska Moving Picture Corp. while on location at the entrance to McKinley National Park. *Photo courtesy of Anchorage Museum.*

The struggles of former years will once again be fought by real veterans of the early days, many of them still re-taining and wearing the identical garments and packs, such as jackets, parkas, fur hats and pack boards used by their owners during the stampede days over the great

Night scene at Girdwood while filming *The Cheechakos. Photo courtesy of Anchorage Museum.*

Chilkoot Pass. Tandem dog teams will once again hit the trail, with the Yukon sled in prominence. The vast illumination will portray sled loads of supplies of flour, bacon, salt, beans, sugar, coffee, tobacco and other bare necessities used by the prospectors.

The first unit of the great gold rush will terminate a week later at Mile 52, where 300 people, consisting of the cast, assistants, Anchorageites and other Alaskan folks, will cross the mountain lying directly back of Bartlett glacier, garbed and outfitted true to the minutest detail to that of 1898.

Many Anchorage citizens joined the human chain climbing Bartlett Glacier, and the directors expressed pride that they could "secure many of the identical men who made the hazardous trip in the early days to once again make the journey for posterity."[50]

Sourdoughs ascending Bartlett Glacier during filming of *The Cheechakos. Photo courtesy of Anchorage Museum.*

After these winter scenes were completed, the cast moved back to Anchorage for the filming of interior scenes on four sets constructed in the movie studio. On April 25, the *Anchorage Daily Times* mentioned that the previous day had been devoted to shooting an interior scene in a log cabin where "the wonderful little child star was seen peering through the cold, frosted window, crying to her mother, being carried away from her in a storm by the good-looking, soft-spoken dance hall and gambling proprietor."

After shooting more interior scenes and some ship-board action on the *Alameda*, Anchoragites prepared for the grand finale of filming in their town before the action moved on to Cordova. On May 23, the *Anchorage Daily Times* described the plan for the dance hall scene:

> Production Manager George E. Lewis states the log cabin town which has been in process of construction for the past two weeks, on Third street, will be completed in a few days. ...
>
> The last day on this set will be very spectacular as fire breaks out in the dance hall during the height of festivities, from which the blaze spreads rapidly to the rest of the buildings, wiping out the entire town. ...
>
> The sensational dance hall scene which will be without a parallel in the moving picture industry, surpassing by far the gorgeous sets of other 'made in the states' Alaskan pictures, will be taken next week, starting possibly on

Gold rush town constructed on west Third Avenue during filming of *The Cheechakos*. *Photo courtesy of Anchorage Museum.*

Wednesday or Thursday. Many Alaskans throughout the territory signified their intentions months ago to participate in this mammoth set. Some are already here, a few will arrive from Nenana and Fairbanks on the next train and word has been received from Cordova that oldtimers and sourdoughs from that vicinity will be present.

It will take at least a full week, working at night, to take this scene, in which from 125 to 300 Alaskan actors will wax merry on the spacious dance hall floor, take chances at the wicked gambling tables and down enough drinks at the big, long bar to float a battleship.

Gold rush town burning during filming of *The Cheechakos*. *Photo courtesy of Anchorage Museum.*

While the Anchorage paper was extolling the picture, Editor Thompson of the *Fairbanks News-Miner* chided Lathrop for "falling for" this "Outside Stuff."[51] Lathrop, however, prophesied that the production would be a great success in a letter to a Seattle friend:

> Personally, I try not to be prejudiced by my interest in the picture, but to be even more critical than the most exacting sourdough when it comes to accuracy of detail and the reproduction of Old Alaska. And at that, I'm telling you that when 'The Cheechakos' is released, you'll see one of the biggest production of the year. ...
>
> We must depend on old timers like yourself, former Alaskans, to explain the pronunciation and definition of

'Cheechakos'. It's a word unknown in the East and middle west today. It stands, more than any other one word, for Alaska. That's why we chose it for our releasing title. And within a month after our picture is released, I hope it will be a household word throughout the country."[52]

Lathrop further explained the title to the editor of *The Alaska Weekly*:

'Cheechako' —pronounced 'Chee-Cha-Ka' — is an Alaska Indian word, meaning 'Person who walks on his heels,' or one used to wearing heels on his shoes, which makes a difference in the way one walks. In other words, those who are used to heels do not walk the same as those wearing moccasins or mukluks. 'Cheechako' was first used in 1896 in Juneau, and the name caught the popular fancy until it was generally employed throughout the northland. In 1898, the word took on a newer and somewhat different interpretation, meaning: A Newcomer or Alaskan Tenderfoot.[53]

After the filming of the dance hall scene on June 7, the log village overlooking Cook Inlet was burned and the cast departed for Cordova to shoot action on Eyak Lake, Abercrombie Rapids and Childs Glacier. Cordova, noted for rain, treated the cast with an unprecedented two weeks of sunny weather, during which the glacier calved gigantic icebergs, causing waves that occasionally drenched the cameramen.[54] President Warren Harding visited the production location after driving the final spike on the Alaska Railroad.[55]

In an interview with the *Los Angeles Sunday Times* the Danish leading lady, Eva Gordon, described the strenuous and dangerous final scene on Childs Glacier: "I was glad I had the knack of snowshoeing stowed away as a memory of my working days in Copenhagen, although that didn't help me greatly when I slipped into a crevasse where I spent four snowy hours before the company could get me dug out. I brought out six frozen toes to remember the experience by, too." Actually Miss Gordon brought back more mementos from Alaska: a four-month-old bear cub, presented to her in

Anchorage; a half-wolf-half-malamute dog, the gift of Cordova; and 170 logs, "ready to be built into a distinctive Hollywood bungalow, reminiscent and typical of Alaska."[56]

Finale of *The Cheechakos* filmed on Childs Glacier near Cordova. *Photo courtesy of Anchorage Museum.*

When the filming of *The Cheechakos* was completed, Lathrop proudly announced to the *Los Angeles Times*: "From the governor of Alaska down to the oldest sourdough our 30,000 inhabitants are vitally interested, all are contributing their part toward the success of this, the first motion picture feature ever filmed in Alaska."[57] On August 9, 1923, the *Cordova Daily Times* announced the contribution of one outstanding Alaskan:

> As a crowning touch of glory and realism, Sidney Laurence, artist of national and international renown, has consented to paint a series of six pictures of Alaskan scenes. These, reproduced on the screen in their natural colors, by the "Prisma" process, will carry the art titles for *The Cheechakos*, and these alone would place this feature where it belongs, in the class of super-productions. ...
>
> The six paintings, with their titles will be: A panoramic mountainous landscape, entitled, "Alaska"; "The Great

White Silence", entitled, "Pure and Beautiful, She Has Stood for Ages, the Great White Silence of the Universe"; Mt. McKinley, entitled, "A Land of Majestic, Snow-capped Peaks, Guarding Fortunes of Untold Wealth"; the glaciers, entitled, "For Centuries Her Crashing Glaciers Have Thundered Defiance to All Who Would Seek Her Hidden Riches"; northern lights, entitled, "From Out of This Unknown Northland a Whisper Came"; canyon and rapids, entitled, "Into That Invincible Onrush of Maddening Confusion Swept the Forerunners, the Mighty Pioneers of the Great Empire Unborn."

Cast of *The Cheechakos* with Cap Lathrop in front row, second from the left. *Photo courtesy of Anchorage Museum.*

When the final editing was done, Lathrop personally took charge of the distribution of the film. In early November *The Cheechakos* was presented to a group of critics and artists in Los Angeles, followed by showings to invited guests in Portland and Seattle. The first Alaska presentations in Anchorage on December 11 and 12 were viewed by many men and women who took part in the filming. The film was then shown in the other Alaska cities on the Empress circuit.

Press releases were complementary, describing Alaska's first-born motion picture in "unstinted words of praise",[58] and *Holly Leaves,* a weekly Hollywood newspaper ran a front page article about Captain A.E. Lathrop, the Alaska theatrical magnate, who forgot his oil fields and seven thriving theaters to join in the "arduous task of selecting locations, picking characters, and drafting sets for the picture, produced three thousand miles from every accessory and convenience." The article went on to describe how Lathrop gave his time, energy and capital, frequently declaring that "the picture would be finished even if he had to give his undershirt", and further praised him for "his unwavering faith in the territory, for his greatest beneficence has been to strengthen his associates in a loyalty to the land of their adoption."[59]

The praise was welcomed, but Lathrop still needed to market *The Cheechakos* to satisfy his investors. On December 29, Lathrop and McDonald left for New York City where they hoped to show the film to critics and sell it to the highest bidder. Two months later the *Anchorage Daily Times* announced that *The Cheechakos* had been sold to the Pathe-International Film Company. Terms of the sale were not made public, but McDonald assured the *Anchorage Daily Times* that "all the stockholders in the company will be well pleased with the returns on their investment." In an interview with the newspaper, he described the New York negotiations:

"No one will know what a man is up against when he tries to sell a picture in New York. I have been up against a lot of hard deals in my life, but this one was a bear. ...

We, I mean Lathrop, Lewis Moomaw, and myself, had so many obstacles thrown in our paths in the way of entertainment, that it was really difficult to concentrate our thoughts on the main subject of the picture, but in the end `we put it over.'...

In New York they drove us from pillar to post, but we always came back to the scratch and insisted upon a hearing. After being buffeted about we finally influenced the powers that be to give us a chance to show our goods. We were not salesmen, but just sincere representatives of Alaska and in the end received permission to show the `Cheechakos' at a preliminary held at the Ritz-Carlton hotel in New York. This showing was given on April 22 to the producers only. The picture made a big hit and we were congratulated upon Alaska's efforts.

Later the picture was shown at the White House to a select audience including President Coolidge, General Pershing, Secretary Work, Secretary Hoover and other notables. And on the following day members of the house and senate were favored with a chance to see Alaska as produced on the silver screen.[60]

The Cheechakos was subsequently shown in movie houses throughout the United States. Critics accepted it as a unique production, praising the scenery but discounting the "silly" story.[61] Mae Tinee, critic for the *Chicago Tribune* summed it up in the following comments:

'The Cheechakos' cooks up a whacking old time melodrama that, in between the play acting, portrays in a way you won't forget the absorbing history of our great northwestern territory.

Treachery, shipwreck, a lost child, a betrayed mother, etc. are thrown against natural scenery that makes you catch your breath. Rough men with hearts of gold, gamblers, dance hall girls, dance halls, while used in the unreeling of a movie story, still manage to give you vivid pictures of what the Alaska pioneers did; how they lived; what they were, and the rest of it. ...

The photography is remarkably good, considering that the production had no Klieg lights, painted glass, miniatures, etc., to fall back upon. There are undoubtedly crude spots to this photoplay — though there's an honesty about the production as a whole that makes you like the crudeness.

Perhaps 'The Cheechakos' will come your way. If it does — take a chance and buy a ticket to the show.[62]

Although the movie studio in Anchorage was built with the intent of producing more films, it was soon modified for other uses. On August 6, 1924, the *Anchorage Daily Times* noted that the big movie studio and surrounding grounds were being transformed into an exhibition center to house the Western Alaska Fair over Labor Day weekend. The newspaper commented:

Where formerly the cries of 'kill `em' and 'ready, action, lights, camera' held forth, and actors of the genus homo strutted in fancy costumes, where all Anchorage gathered to see the villain do his 'woist', and the hero do the villain 'foist', four-legged actors of Alaska of various kinds and species will hold forth soon.

The building never housed another movie production, but was used as a community center for Anchorage for many years.

Several other movies were filmed in Alaska the following year, but Cap Lathrop had other enterprises on his mind — Standard Oil was drilling on adjoining Coal Bay leases, and the Alaska Railroad needed his Healy River coal.

HEALY RIVER — 1925-1931
A Coal Mine Pays Off

With the fate of *The Cheechakos* in the hands of Associated Exhibitors, a subsidiary of Pathe, Captain Lathrop prepared to take advantage of new opportunities in resource development. President Warren Harding had finally opened Alaskan lands for mineral leasing after years of closure during the Wilson administration. The boom-town of Kanatak sprang up overnight near where Lathrop had drilled for oil twenty years before, but Standard Oil was no more successful in 1924 than Lathrop had been in 1905. Kanatak was soon just another Alaska ghost town.

Healy River coal mine in 1922. *Photo courtesy of Anchorage Museum.*

With failure in oil speculation and less than anticipated revenues from *The Cheechakos*, Lathrop was again fortunate to have diversified holdings. The Empress theater chain continued to supply him ample revenue to proceed with development of the Healy River coal mines. On August 6, 1924, the *Anchorage Daily Times* printed the following report of the annual stockholders' meeting of the Healy River Coal Mines Corporation at which Lathrop was re-elected president:

> At the directors' meeting the following day extensive improvements to the equipment at the mine were planned. The Gordon outfit of two 60 horsepower boilers and engines was purchased from the Northern Commercial company and will be installed at the mine. Pouring of concrete for the boiler walls and the engine slabs was started today at the mine. With this added equipment the Healy Mines will rank among the best equipped in Alaska. The corporation is also building a new tipple with a shaker stirring system. ...
>
> The Healy River corporation has run its main tunnel through for 1000 feet to their last vein, crossing five other veins and tapping the latter. ...
>
> Another improvement in the equipment of the corporation will be the establishment of substantial coal bunkers in Fairbanks. ... The bunkers will hold enough coal for the use of the creek operators and the local sales in Fairbanks.
>
> Austin E. Lathrop, president of the organization, will remain at the mines and at Fairbanks until the completion of the improvements.

Lathrop was again doing what he enjoyed the most — hard outdoor construction work at the mine. Although almost 60 years old, he was strong and continued to enjoy excellent health. He remained at the mine until early November when he returned to Anchorage to supervise improvements at the Lathrop building, including the installation of up-to-date equipment, described in the *Anchorage Daily Times* on November 12, 1924:

> Another innovation for the comfort and efficiency of

the Lathrop building is the installation of an electrical stoker or 'automatic fireman'. This apparatus, operated by a thermostatically controlled electric motor, by means of a worm screw arrangement automatically feeds mine run Healy river coal into the firebox under the boiler, and keeps the temperature even throughout the day. An electric time clock also sets the motor driven apparatus in action in the early hours of the morning. A five hundred pound hopper contains the coal to be fed. A coal bin with a capacity of three car loads has been constructed in the lot at the rear of the Lathrop building.

When these renovations were finished, Lathrop left Alaska on a business trip, but was called back to Anchorage by the serious illness and eventual death of Ruby DeGraff from tuberculous meningitis. The 44-year-old Miss DeGraff, a capable and efficient businesswoman in her own right, had been Lathrop's confidential secretary for 14 years. In an attempt to reach her bedside, Lathrop transferred from the southbound steamship *Northwestern* on the sea outside Cordova to a gas boat for Seward and then chartered an Alaska Railroad train to bring him to Anchorage.[63] After accompanying Miss DeGraff's body to Seattle for burial, Lathrop proceeded to make business trips to Portland, California and eventually New York, looking after interests connected with distribution of *The Cheechakos*.[64]

As soon as spring breakup was over and a new bridge over the Healy River completed in late May, Lathrop returned to the Healy River mine with a mining engineer from Seattle to draw up plans for more buildings and a new tipple equipped with electrically driven shaker screens to eliminate all foreign matter. Although the Healy River mine already ranked as the largest coal producer in the territory, with an output of 135 tons daily, Lathrop was intent upon assuring that the mine would be as modern and well- equipped as any mine in the state of Washington.[65] *The Alaska Weekly* announced on November 13, 1925, that the new tipple was in place above five standard gauge railroad tracks and that the management was installing an electric locomotive to work in the mine. The article further described the status of development at the mine:

The buildings are all heated by steam, electric lighted, and very warm and comfortable. They include a large dormitory, mess house, freight shed, superintendent's dwelling, bath house, storehouse, office, and a very complete and up-to-date power plant. Housed in the power plant there are two 60-horsepower Penn boilers and one 30- horsepower Penn boiler. All boilers and machinery are in concrete foundations, eliminating all vibration.

Lathrop spent the entire summer of 1925 at the Healy River Mine and was still there in December when the stockholders again elected him president at their annual meeting in Fairbanks. The stockholders anticipated increased demand for coal as soon as the Fairbanks Exploration Company, a big gold mining concern, started operations.[66]

With major construction completed at the mine, Lathrop looked toward Fairbanks for his next building project. On June 25, 1926 *The Alaska Weekly* announced that "Captain Austin E. Lathrop, motion picture magnate of Alaska, head of the Healy River Coal Company, and big businessman of the territory has definitely decided on the erection of a great hotel and apartment in connection with a moving picture house in the city of Fairbanks." In planning to construct this four-story building of reinforced concrete, Lathrop was taking a risk. Up to this time no one had dared to construct concrete buildings in that permafrost area for fear that shifting of the ground would crack the foundations. Lathrop hired George R. Purvis, who had built the Empress Theatres in Anchorage and Cordova, as his contractor and construction on the 600-seat theater began in April 1927.[67] The building, which included 100 hotel rooms on the upper floors, was completed by the end of the summer. On August 25, 1927, the Empress Theatre hosted a gala opening ceremony, featuring musical selections on the first Kimball pipe organ in Fairbanks. The concrete building withstood the ravages of Arctic winters, proving that modern construction was feasible in Fairbanks. Lathrop was amused to watch federal inspectors come up each year to examine his building for cracks. Eventually they were convinced and used concrete in the new Fairbanks federal buildings.[68] Years later the concrete walls of the Empress

Theatre saved part of the business district from destruction in a mid-winter fire.

Rumors that offices and presses of the *Fairbanks Daily News-Miner* would occupy space in the Empress theater building were premature in 1927[69], but two years later, on November 8, 1929, a front page box in the *News-Miner* proclaimed:

As the press run ended on yesterday's News-Miner, an old chapter closed and a new opened in the history of the publication and its parent, the Tanana Publishing Co., Inc.

The interest of W.F. Thompson, dating back through the years to the amalgamation of the News and the Miner and perpetuated since his death three years ago by Mrs. Thompson, passed to a new helmsman, Capt. Austin E. Lathrop.

The transaction came about through a desire by Mrs. Thompson to close her business interest, and through a confidence in the future prosperity of Interior Alaska on the part of Capt. Lathrop.

The new president of the Tanana Publishing Co. scarcely needs an introduction. A pioneer in the upbuilding of communities on the Alaskan coast, through transportation, banking and theaters, he cast his lot with the Interior when his Empress theaters in Cordova and Anchorage grew to include Fairbanks.

Greater interest came to include the presidency and general managership of the Healy River Coal Corp., with extensive development of its mines and facilities at Suntrana, Republican National Committeemanship, Alaskan representative of the Aero Arctic Society, president of the International Highway Association and other endeavors allied with the march of Alaskan progress.

During these years Lathrop exuded confidence in the future of Interior Alaska and established Fairbanks as his official residence although he continued to oversee his business interests in Anchorage and Cordova.[70] Since Lathrop was well-known and respected throughout Alaska, Republican friends urged him to enter the political arena again and run for National Committeeman in 1928. The election was close and not finally decided in Lathrop's favor until after his return from the Republican National Convention in Kansas City.

Austin Lathrop, Dr. Will Chase, and James Wickersham at the 1928 Republican National Convention. *Photo courtesy of UAA*

Prior to the convention Lathrop and Judge James Wickersham agreed to present a united Republican front although they represented opposing factions of the party.[71] For 20 years Wickersham had waged a personal vendetta against the Kennecott Copper Corporation, the Copper River and Northwestern Railroad and the Alaska Steamship Company which he accused of being controlled by "big interests" intent on gobbling up the natural resources of Alaska. Lathrop, who helped the Alaska Syndicate develop Cordova, continued friendly association with the managers of these enterprises and must have resented the bitter personal attacks that Wickersham made on personal friends such as George Hazelet of Cordova and Thomas Marquam of Fairbanks. Wickersham did not attack Lathrop personally, but in his diary he repeatedly identified Lathrop as his main antagonist within the Republican party.[72]

The temporary truce during the Republican National Convention did not last for long. When Lathrop became the publisher of the *Fairbanks Daily News-Miner* he acquired a means for opposing Wickersham's election as delegate to Congress in 1930. The editorials by Bernard M. Stone praised Attorney General John Rustgard, Wickersham opponent in the 1930 Republican primary, and criticized Wickersham for his allegiance with William Paul in lawsuits to establish Native claims to Southeastern Alaska lands.[73] The paper printed the text of Rustgard speeches denouncing Wickersham for halting the industrial development of Alaska.[74] Although Lathrop, as National Committeeman, openly supported Rustgard, Wickersham retained enough statewide support to win the election. For the next two years the two Republican factions fought each other for patronage in appointments to federal positions in Alaska. After the landslide election of Franklin Roosevelt in 1932 ended Republican domination of Alaska politics, Lathrop turned over the position of national committeeman to Edward A. Rasmuson, head of the National Bank of Alaska, a representative of the opposing faction within the Republican party.[75] While a Republican, George Parks, was still governor of Alaska in 1932, he appointed Lathrop a regent of the University of Alaska. The farm boy who never finished high school took an active part in the development of higher education in Alaska for the next 18 years.

CORDOVA — 1932-1936
New Industry for the Copper City

Lathrop had some new associates working with him in 1932 when he retired from the political arena. The death of Ruby DeGraff eight years before had left him without a personal secretary, and failing health had forced his Anchorage manager, A.J. Hewitt, to retire to Arizona.[76] Miriam Dickey, a young University of Washington journalism graduate, came to Lathrop's Seattle office in 1931 looking for work. Lathrop initially thought her too young to work for him, but then decided to give her a chance and sent her home with a typewriter. Although Miss Dickey claims that she was never officially hired, she soon became Lathrop's confidential secretary, business advisor, hostess, and surrogate daughter.[77]

In spite of nationwide depression Lathrop's Fairbanks business interests flourished. The Healy River mines produced more coal than the combined output of all the other mines in the Territory,[78] and Lathrop soon began construction of modern bunkers in Fairbanks that would be sufficiently large to accommodate a supply of coal for the town and for gold mines on neighboring creeks.[79] Lathrop continued to work actively in the coal mine and was hospitalized briefly in June 1932 for treatment of leg injuries sustained at Suntrana.[80] Gold remained a stable commodity during the depression, so gold mining in Alaska prospered. On October 14, 1932, *The Alaska Weekly* announced that Captain Lathrop was leasing a group of gold claims on Cleary Creek, 25 miles from Fairbanks.

The economic condition of Cordova was not as bright. The Kennecott mines were running out of high-grade copper ore, and the low price for copper precipitated a temporary closure of the mines and disruption of service on the Copper River and Northwestern Railroad. In an effort to stabilize the Cordova banks, Lathrop, the principal stockholder in the First Bank of Cordova, and E.A. Rasmuson, head of the Bank of Alaska chain, met in Cordova in the summer of 1932 to arrange an amalgamation of the assets of the First Bank of Cordova and the Cordova branch of the Bank of Alaska. On September 8, the *Cordova Daily Times* noted that the business of the two banks was being conducted at the banking quarters of the First Bank of Cordova.

Increased involvement in the First Bank of Cordova made it necessary for Lathrop to spend more time at the Copper River port that he had helped to build 25 years before. In October 1932 Lathrop and Miss Dickey were joined in Cordova by John H. Clawson, a former Internal Revenue collector from Seattle, who was assuming the management of Lathrop's Alaska interests.[81] While many Cordovans still dreamed of a day when copper mines would again work at full capacity and the Copper River and Northwestern Railroad trains would run both summer and winter, Lathrop realized that fishing would be the future industry in Cordova and airplanes the transportation link to the rest of Alaska. Improvements in the town's airport and cannery facilities and modifications in fishery regulations would be essential for the economic survival of Cordova.

In order to promote Cordova's cause Lathrop and James L. Galen traveled to Washington D.C.in February 1933 as representatives of the Cordova Chamber of Commerce.[82] Galen had been a friend and business associate of Lathrop's since 1915 when he bought the Cordova transfer company that Lathrop started. The two men were also associated in the McKinley Park Tourist and Transportation Company which was building facilities in McKinley Park to serve the growing tourist trade.[83] Results of their lobbying were soon evident. *The Cordova Daily Times* announced on March 2 that Galen had persuaded the fishing commissioner Henry O'Malley to extend the clam digging season in Cordova, and several days later O'Malley opened the Bering River fishing area that had been closed for five years. At the request of the Chamber, Lathrop discussed the dredging of Cordova's small boat harbor with the United States Engineer's office in Seattle. Before returning to Cordova in April, the two men stopped in Juneau to rally support for an appropriation to build an airport for Cordova.[85]

Cordova fire that damaged the Empress Theatre around 1932. *Photo courtesy of UAA.*

While Lathrop and Galen were traveling in the East, two things further strengthened Lathrop's commitment to Cordova. A fire destroyed part of downtown Cordova and damaged the Lathrop apartment building on February 24, and, in early March, President Franklin D. Roosevelt proclaimed a bank holiday. The First Bank of Cordova was able to prove its stability and reopen largely because Lathrop had Clawson make an emergency airplane trip to Seattle with securities to serve as collateral for a loan from the Pacific National Bank.[85]

While passing through Cordova in early May on his return from the trip, Lathrop proudly displayed a map of possible routes for a Pacific Yukon highway that he was promoting.[86] He also arranged for repair of the fire- damaged Lathrop apartments and the installation of a new Kewanee boiler to provide the building with one of the most modern and efficient heating plants in Alaska.[87] After another trip to Cordova in mid July, newspapers throughout the territory announced that, under a new reorganization, Captain A.E. Lathrop was assuming the presidency of the First Bank of Cordova.[88]

With this increased responsibility for financial stability in

Cordova, Lathrop set out to stimulate new industry. The Territorial legislature narrowly passed an appropriation of $15,000 for the Cordova airport and construction was about to begin when Lathrop addressed a Chamber Commerce luncheon as reported in the August 30, 1933 *Cordova Daily Times*:

> Although duck hunting made a serious inroad on the Chamber of Commerce luncheon attendance today, one of the most spirited meetings in weeks took place when Capt. A.E. Lathrop initiated a move for the construction of a modern all-metal hangar on the new aviation field.
>
> The fact that the field itself was assured did not mean that Cordova's responsibility toward its future aviation business was terminated, pointed out Captain Lathrop. As important as a place to land planes was a place to house them, he said, and this item was becoming more paramount as aviation companies in Alaska were investing in larger and more expensive planes. ... In his earnestness to have his suggestions carried out he said he would match dollar for dollar any amount the city would put up for a hangar.
>
> He spoke again of the tremendous importance of aviation in Alaska. He reiterated once more that fliers in the interior of the Territory were anxious to make their coast headquarters here but that they hesitated to do so without hangar facilities. He said for the enlightenment of the Chamber and others that he would bring back estimates of the cost of construction of an eighty by one hundred foot hangar when he visits the states in the near future on a business trip.

Lathrop and Clawson returned from their five week trip to Seattle, Portland, Chicago, Washington D.C., and New York with reports of an upturn in the economic status of the country and increased interest in Alaska's fishing and gold mining. In a Juneau interview Lathrop expressed belief that the National Recovery Act would be the "salvation of the country."[89] True to his promise Lathrop presented the Cordova Chamber of Commerce with a plan for construction of a hangar at the new airfield. The *Cordova Daily Times* reported on November 8:

Capt. A.E. Lathrop said he would procure $20,000 toward a hangar if the city of Cordova would raise $5,000. Ten thousand of this money, Capt. Lathrop said, was his personal donation while the other $10,000 would be available from another unnamed source. The hangar, if it is erected, will be of the most modern type, said Capt. Lathrop. It will be of all-steel construction and of ample size to house the largest plane.

Later that month the Cordova newspaper announced the arrival in town of a second Kewanee steam boiler to be provide steam heat to buildings in the Cordova central business district and described the planned installation:

The boiler will likely be placed in position in the basement of the Lathrop building tomorrow, where the cement foundations have already been installed. It was necessary to remove a section of the wall to allow the new plant to enter the building. An automatic coal stoker will be used to fuel the plant and Alaska coal will be used entirely, states Capt. Lathrop. Pipes have already been installed under the city streets to the Mutual building and the hospital building and other firms will probably later take their heat from this plant. A smaller boiler was previously installed in the Lathrop building to supply heat to the building proper."[90]

The *Anchorage Daily Times* took note of the new heating system in a January 23 editorial, entitled "Cordova's Example":

Cordova is to be congratulated on this progressive movement. The new plant should supply heat at a minimum. At the same time it will do something of more importance to Alaskans. It will keep the money which goes into the purchase of coal at home.

Capt. A.E. Lathrop, outstanding captain of industry, a man who makes his money here and reinvests it here, is understood to be largely if not chiefly responsible for Cordova's enterprise. More men of this type are needed to put Alaska permanently on the map and stop her from being milked of her wealth."

When Lathrop acquired controlling interest in the First Bank of Cordova, the bank held outstanding loans to various Cordova businesses. In the interest of improving the banks financial status, Lathrop decided to pay off several of these loans and as a result further broadened the diversity of his investments. In March 1933 Alaska newspapers announced that "all interests in Laurie Brothers, Cordova clothiers and general merchandise dealers, have been disposed of to Capt. A.E. Lathrop, Cordova and Anchorage businessman."[91] About the same time Lathrop acquired part ownership of the Glacier Packing Company.

With these new businesses in Cordova, in addition to the theaters and apartments in Anchorage and Fairbanks, the *Fairbanks News-Miner*, and the Healy River coal mines, Lathrop was always traveling. Weather prevented him from flying to Cordova for the dedication of the new airport on June 21, 1934, but he arrived several days later to oversee construction of the Lathrop hangar. By the end of 1934 two scheduled air carriers, the Cordova Air Service and Gillam Airways, were operating out of the Cordova airport and air service had proved invaluable as a means of bringing stricken people to medical care.[92] Business at the airport picked up in late October when the Copper River and Northwestern Railroad closed for the winter.

Lathrop Company carpenters returned to Cordova in late February 1935 to construct a new cannery building and cannery offices for the Glacier Packing Company.[93] Lathrop's new involvement in the seafood industry was recognized in Washington D.C. with his appointment to the National Fisheries Board in March 1935.[94]

When Lathrop himself returned to Cordova in late spring he presented a new construction plan to the Chamber of Commerce. The small machine shop in the Lathrop hangar was not adequate to meet the need for aircraft repair and maintenance so Lathrop arranged a 50 year lease on adjoining land to erect large machine shop. The *Cordova Daily Times* gave the following report of construction progress on September 9, 1935:

> Amidst the singing of saws, intonation of hammer and adze, rattle of lumber and thud of rock and earth as a force of nine workmen are 'hitting the ball', the new ma-

chine shop, being built in connection with the modern hangar recently built by Capt. A.E. Lathrop, is beginning to take shape.

When finished Cordova will have one of the most up-to-date airfields in Alaska.

The machine shop will have the same dimensions as the hangar — 60x60 feet, and be built of wood frame, steel and glass. ...

The hangar and machine shop is what may be termed a 'beau geste' of Captain Lathrop. It is a response to the urge to build and give vent to those energies which Captain Lathrop has displayed throughout his career and through which he has left his hand-mark on the development history of Alaska.

Having never kicked over the ladder on which he climbed, nothing pleases Captain Lathrop more than to give personal direction to the work, and to take a hand now and then. All of which evokes good- natured raillery by his intimates.

At the end of the construction season, Lathrop traveled to Seattle for his annual winter business trip and again spoke in glowing terms about the future of development in Alaska during an interview with *The Alaska Weekly*. He also spoke of his growing disillusion with the New Deal and the growth of the federal bureaucracy.[95]

Lathrop arrived back in Cordova on April 1 and the *Cordova Daily Times* commented that his health was excellent and, though over 70, he still had his "old time vigor."[96] He immediately went to the Glacier Packing Company to take charge of the installation of equipment for a high-speed canning line. On April 6 the newspaper described the renovation of the cannery:

The Glacier Sea Foods, under the direct supervision of one of its owners, Capt. Austin E. Lathrop, is being completely rebuilt from the floor up. It is located at the approach of the Ocean Dock. The large building with its 100-foot front and its adjacent office building was erected last summer but was not completed. ...

The Glacier Sea Foods plant will be one of the finest to be found anywhere in the salmon canning industry. Cleanliness in packing is to be paramount. The entire interior is to be sealed with tongue-and- groove lumber and will be finished in heavy white enamel. The building is well provided with windows so that there will be a maximum of light at all times. Larger windows along the front will allow a full view of the interior to passerby and a walk and railing along the side of the building will allow spectators to watch the canning process without going into the plant. Visitors will at all times be welcome inside, however.

At present carpenters are concentrating on the construction of heavy fish bins, the sides of which are oiled to facilitate washing. The company is providing an ample number of bins so that at no time will fish have to be piled too deeply.

The future of the fishing industry in Cordova looked bright in the summer of 1936. Canneries were working at full capacity, the Senate passed an appropriation for development of the Cordova small boat harbor, and the town looked forward to construction of a cold storage plant as soon as the harbor project was completed.[97] Cordova had a future ahead in spite of the final closure of the Kennecott mines and the Copper River and Northwestern Railroad in 1938.

FAIRBANKS — 1937-1941
KFAR — Key For Alaska's Riches

After spending the winter attending to business interests in Seattle and other stateside cities, Captain Lathrop arrived in Cordova on May 19, 1937. News of extensive flooding in Fairbanks prompted him to proceed immediately to the interior city to assess the extent of damage there. Within a week the *Cordova Daily Times* announced Lathrop's plan to erect a four-story concrete building in downtown Fairbanks as a "substantial expression of faith in the future of Fairbanks and Alaska."

The publishing plant and offices of the *Fairbanks News-Miner* would occupy the ground floor, and 24 deluxe two, three and four room apartments would fill the next two floors. The Cordova paper went on to describe the new equipment on order for the printing plant:

> The new newspaper equipment will include a new Model 14 Morgenthaler Linotype, the latest thing in that wonderful mechanical marvel, to supplement other machines now in service. There also will be a brand new Cox-o-Type web press for printing the daily paper in any number of pages, with neatness and dispatch, turning out 3600 16-page papers in an hour. A new Kelly II automatic job press and smaller presses will complete the press battery.
>
> All metal type cases, latest in fonts of type, makeup conveniences, paper cutters and the like will give the News-Miner something of which all Alaskans will be proud.[98]

Lathrop spent most of the next three summers in Fairbanks personally supervising construction of the $500,000 Lathrop Building. The newspaper plant on the ground floor was completed in 1937 and the apartments, equipped with solid Philippine mahogany doors and built-in china cabinets, were finished the following year. Lathrop spent a lot of time in Fairbanks so he reserved one of the apartments for himself, but later turned it over to a newly-married employee who couldn't find a place to live and moved in with the building superintendent.[99]

Three floors of the building were completed and occupied in 1938 but plans for the fourth floor were still uncertain. Finally in June of that year Lathrop received the news he had been waiting for — permission to construct a radio station in Fairbanks. Miriam Dickey had been the first to suggest a radio station and Lathrop responded with enthusiasm. Before plunging into the radio project, Lathrop located every mine and outpost in the vast Alaskan interior within the station's expected range. *Time* magazine reported in the June 12, 1939

Captain Lathrop with his "right hand man", Miriam Dickey. *Photo courtesy of Anchorage Museum.*

issue that "for expected sponsors the census showed a potential audience of some 25,000, with a per capita buying power five times that of the average U.S. consumer and little else to do in the evenings but listen to the radio." In spite of its obvious commercial value, Lathrop considered the radio station to be a gift to the people of Alaska and invested a lot more in it than he ever hoped to recover. In an interview with the *Seattle Post-Intelligencer* before leaving for Alaska in May 1939 he explained: "Yes, the people of Alaska have given to me and my ventures for forty-three years and I think this is about the best way I can show my appreciation."[100]

By the end of September the fourth floor of the Lathrop Building was filled with offices and studios for KFAR, whose call letters signify "Key for Alaska's Riches." Five miles northwest of Fairbanks on Farm Loop Road a new modernistic white-walled building housed the transmitting equipment and the *Fairbanks News-Miner* likened the 300-foot vertical antenna to a "totem pole significant of latest twentieth century advance in entertainment and education of interior Alaska."

The official dedication of KFAR took place on Sunday, October 1, 1939, and the following day the *News-Miner* reported:

Riding the crest of 1000 watts' power, the Midnight Sun Broadcasting Company's station in Fairbanks boomed its dedicatory message to every Alaska nook and cranny and to sensitive receiving equipment throughout the world.

Overshadowed only by the multiple aspects of wide civic beneficence in the historic — for Alaska — opening was the momentous, though unsought, personal triumph won by Captain Austin E. Lathrop.

High emotional pitch of the broadcast ascended to climax with a finale not "in the script" presentation to the hardy Alaskan of a giant bronze plaque.

There was not a dry

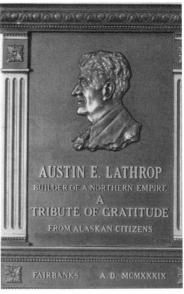

Bust of "Austin E. Lathrop, builder of a northern empire. A tribute of gratitude from Alaskan citizens. Fairbanks. A.D. MCMXXXIX."
Photo courtesy of Anchorage Museum.

eye in the house when Southall Pfaud, representing immediately the residents of Fairbanks and the citizenry of Alaska at large, called for the unveiling of the plaque before the totally unsuspecting gaze of the one-time steamer captain.

Inscribed on the 100-pound trophy is: Austin E. Lathrop, Builder of a Northern Empire. A Tribute of Gratitude From Alaskan Citizens. Fairbanks A.D. MCMXXXIX. Above the inscription is a bust of Captain Lathrop modeled by Pietro Vigna, Fairbanks artist, from a photograph.

Promptly at 7 P.M. the station manager proclaimed, "KFAR is on the air!" and flashbulbs flared and movie cameras whirred for the next 90 minutes during which many distinguished guests were brought to the microphone. Lathrop, as president of the Midnight Sun Broadcasting Company, was the first to speak, stating simply: "To all my friends in Alaska and the States, I can only say this is the happiest day of my life. I hope you will derive as great a pleasure from KFAR's programs as we have all experienced in building and planning this station. ... I feel very proud that I have been privileged to bring KFAR to my people."

The same newspapers that detailed plans for the KFAR dedication announced that another Lathrop building project, the 560-seat Lacey Street Theater, was nearing completion and would be showing motion pictures in about 90 days. Lathrop abandoned the archaic spelling and planned the new theater as a show place of modern equipment and decor, as described in the newspaper on September 30, 1939:

> Modeled in modern steamline motif, the white-walled edifice will present a decorative plaster facade centered by an entrance styled in Italian travertine marble. Plaster decorations, inside and out, are the work of Joseph Jefferson and his assistant, Ray Duncan.
>
> Jefferson has supervised the decorating of theaters throughout the West, including many of Seattle's principal show houses.
>
> Ceilings will be lined in patterned acoustic cork. The building will be air-conditioned throughout, under a roof of

three-inch fireproof thermax whose weather-hardiness will be bolstered by five-ply built-up roofing. ... A high percentage of material and supplies for the Lacey Street Theater has been purchased from or through Fairbanks firms.

Lacey Street Theater under construction. *Photo courtesy of Anchorage Museum.*

This last sentence demonstrates Lathrop's resolve to invest, whenever possible, in the local economy. As his personal wealth increased people frequently urged him to invest in enterprises outside of Alaska, but he continued to insist that the money generated in Alaska should be plowed back into the economy of the Territory. Money itself meant little to Lathrop except as a means to build something new.[101] An article in the April 1940 issue of *Alaska Life* described how Lathrop used the profit from the Healy River coal mine to assist in establishing a firm economic base for Interior Alaska:

> It is certain that the Fairbanks Exploration Company would not have invested millions in the Tanana region if economical power had not been available. And that's where Lathrop and his coal entered the picture. For upon his price per carload, delivered in Fairbanks, estimates for mining costs were based. A power plant was designed and built to meet the specifications of the Healy River product. Power lines were stretched across the hills. The Chatanika Ditch and its many extensions were completed. Dredges were built. Hydraulic operations were mapped out and Fairbanks started tearing down its log houses and

commenced building for the future. Fairbanks had passed the crisis and was returning to health and vigor.

An index to the character of Cap Lathrop is a little known incident that occurred in the office of the Fairbanks Exploration Company a number of years ago. Lathrop had an ironclad contract to deliver a large tonnage of coal to the F.E. at a specified price that was agreeable to both parties. Deliveries were being made regularly and on the date required. One morning Cap called on the F.E. executives, asked if everything was satisfactory with the quality of the coal and its delivery. He was informed that it was meeting specifications and there were no complaints.

'Well, I wonder it you would mind if I reduced the price? You see, we have been able to mine the coal at Healy River more efficiently and more economically than I thought possible. I'll still make the percentage of profit I had figured on, even at the reduced price. With lower operation costs in mining you no doubt will be able to expand your field of activity in the Fairbanks region.

The Healy River mine will be satisfied with a lower price. You can increase your area of prospecting and the people of Fairbanks will benefit by more business and more employment.

The mining executives looked for a 'catch'. There wasn't any.[102]

In spite of his belief in free enterprise, Lathrop did not welcome competition. Part of his motivation in building the Lacey Street Theater may have been to keep anyone else from building a movie house to compete with the Empress. He also used his influence to stifle competition with another of his financial interests, the Olympia brewery. Before prohibition Lathrop had been the Alaska distributor for Olympia beer and he subsequently invested in the Seattle firm to help his friend Peter Schmidt during prohibition. In 1933 when the sale of beer was legal again, Lathrop was elected a director of the Olympia firm and granted the distributorship for Alaska. Although not a heavy drinker, Lathrop always specified Olympia when he entered a bar and gave the proprietor a tongue lashing if his favorite brand was not readily available.[104] Lathrop's influence in Alaska was sufficient to prevent small breweries from establishing markets.[105]

With so many varied activities, Lathrop needed to employ a number of people with specialized talents. He knew all his employees personally, from executives to coal miners, and considered them part of his family. Although he rarely interfered with day-to-day management he always knew what was going on, as explained by Georg Nelson Meyers in an article for *Cosmopolitan*:

> His employees know that just because Cap isn't always breathing down their necks is no sign that he doesn't know what's going on. He can tell you how many carloads of stoker coal were taken out at Suntrana yesterday. He can spot a typographical error at ten paces. One day he stopped the cashier in one of his banks in the act of making a loan to a cab driver. "Hell's handles, man" he stormed. "You make many loans like this and you'll have me in the poorhouse yet!" The next day the cabby came in to talk to Cap about the loan. Cap turned to his secretary and said, "Write him a personal check." This baffled the bank cashier. Cap explained it to him: "It wasn't good banking for a bank to make this loan. But I'm not a bank."[106]

When Lathrop entered the radio business he hired two young engineers, Stanton Bennett and August Hiebert, who had worked together previously at a station in Bend, Oregon. The two engineers lived in a specially designed apartment at the transmitter site so that they could be available night and day to solve any technical problems. Lathrop admitted that he did not understand the radio technology but soon after KFAR opened he was visited by a relative who did. Austin Cooley, the son of one of Lathrop's sisters, was Cap's protege. When only 14, young Cooley spent a summer working as a projectionist in Lathrop's first Cordova theater. Two years later, Cooley ran away from home to run a short wave radio station on an island in Southeast Alaska. After Cooley returned from World War I, Lathrop arranged to have him enter Massachusetts Institute of Technology, but the young man preferred to spend his time working on his own to perfect a facsimile machine.[107]

The KFAR engineers understood what Austin Cooley was trying to do. Bennett and Hiebert agreed to help him test his invention, and Lathrop was delighted to have them cooperate with his nephew. Cooley wanted to prove that he could transmit pictures by short wave so the KFAR engineers got licenses to use their amateur radio K7XSB to transmit and receive facsimile with Cooley who manned his own equipment in New York City. Every Sunday morning Hiebert and Bennett would monitor four assigned frequencies to receive pictures transmitted as negatives from which they made 8x10 prints in their own darkroom. According to Hiebert they got remarkable results in spite of poor short wave transmitting conditions in central Alaska.

These experiments with facsimile technology lasted for about a year but ended dramatically on December 7, 1941. That Sunday morning Hiebert woke up early and turned on the short wave in anticipation of transmissions from Cooley. While listening to the short wave radio, Hiebert was the first person in Alaska to hear about the Japanese attack on Pearl Harbor. He immediately informed General Simon Boliver Buckner, the head of military operations in Alaska, who did not receive official word of the attack for several hours. Wartime regulations put an end to short wave transmission at KFAR, but General "Hap" Arnold learned about Cooley's facsimile technology and worked with him to develop a means of transmitting weather maps.[108]

Lathrop's radio station, with its slogan, "From the Top of the World to You," had already become an integral part of life in interior Alaska, transmitting mining information, airplane arrivals and departures, and information about births, deaths and marriages. World War II altered its mission. KFAR soon became the armed services station with increased power and military programing.

WORLD WAR II — 1942-1947

KFAR was not the only part of Lathrop's empire that was changed by the advent of World War II. Shortages of building materials and labor forced him to suspend his two new building projects - a radio station and a new theater in Anchorage. Lathrop planned to make the Fourth Avenue Theater in Anchorage even more luxurious than the Lacey Street Theater, which at the time of its opening in 1940 was proclaimed to be the most expensive theater per seat ever built in the United States.[109]

The Healy River coal mines, however, felt the greatest impact from the war. With Japanese warships threatening shipments from the States, the army and airforce in Alaska relied heavily on Healy River coal. These were Lathrop's most trying days. "The army was hollering for more coal this morning," he complained, "and this afternoon they drafted four more of my miners."[110] To help remedy this situation, Lathrop spent more time at the mines, working alongside the remaining miners. Although over 75 years old, he was still strong and able to do a full day of hard physical work. Fairbanks residents frequently saw him, dressed in mackinaw and shoe-pacs with his battered hat pushed back over wavy white hair, walking to the Alaska Railroad station to take the morning train to Suntrana.[111] Even after the war was over Lathrop continued to work in the mines where he felt most comfortable. He donned more formal clothes for other occasions — gabardines for trips to Anchorage and a dark three-piece suit for meetings with Seattle bankers.

After the war KFAR resumed the function of carrying news

Cap Lathrop boards the train to Healy River coal mine. *Photo courtesy of UAF.*

to the remote mines and villages in Interior Alaska. The November 24, 1946 magazine supplement *This Week* gave the following description of KFAR programing:

> Announcer Stevens has never yet given a play-by-play account of a blanket-tossing contest, but he has broadcast curling matches, midnight baseball played in full sunlight (this is Alaska, remember), and the annual ice break-up on the Tanana River. KFAR's big annual sports broadcast is the Fairbanks winter dog-sled derby.
>
> Station KFAR was originally built because a bronze statue wasn't. In 1936 a town committee asked Austin E. ("Cap") Lathrop, a wealthy Alaskan, to put up money for a statue of a sourdough. "Cap" Lathrop decided that if he was going to do something for Alaska, he'd rather set up

a good radio station. The committee agreed it was a better idea. So KFAR was born.

Today it is better equipped than many in the United States. Its 10,000-watt transmitting power covers a thousand-mile radius. Its programs may reach the North Pole - if there's anyone there who owns a radio.

Music, news and feature programs are KFAR's fare. No soap operas - Alaskans won't put up with them. They don't like singing commercials either.

Classical music gets more requests than swing, but very old popular songs are the top favorites. KFAR is probably the only station in the world that has a library of ancient cylindrical records. Every once in a while they play a few to please lonely old sourdoughs who still stick to song hits like "Wait `Till the Sun Shines, Nellie."

KFAR's favorite listener is the Indian chief who traveled 500 miles to inspect the station. He explained that there was a quarrel among his tribesmen - some said Station KFAR was a real place in Alaska that sent sounds into their radio set; others claimed it was just magic.

Waiting room of KFAR radio station. *Photo courtesy of Anchorage Museum.*

The KFAR announcers, Ed Stevens and Al Bramstedt, conceived the idea of broadcasting the Nenana breakup in 1945. They obtained camping equipment for Bramstedt to use while waiting for the ice to go out and stored it at the station. Lathrop spotted the sleeping bag one day and was told of the plan. "You mean you're going to send that SOB down there on my payroll," Cap exploded. "It may take weeks!" Lathrop didn't forbid the expedition, however. The breakup occurred without undue waiting, and Bramstedt's "floe-by-floe" description was an immediate success.[112]

Bramstedt had the opportunity to give an unanticipated "blow-by-blow" account of a devastating fire that destroyed part of downtown Fairbanks on January 5, 1946. He was working that Saturday night when a fire started in the Co-op Drug Store. Although it was 50 degrees below zero, Bramstedt climbed to the top of the Lathrop Building to broadcast the progress of the fire while Lathrop waited on top of his Empress Theatre building, confident that its concrete walls would stop the fire. Bramstedt would describe the fire until his microphone would freeze. Then he would drop it down the side of the building into a window, and people would bring another one up to him. Lathrop's fireproof concrete-walled theater did stop the flames. Cap was a proud man when he returned to the street and received thanks from people who saw that his building had saved the town.

In 1946 Lathrop was finally able to resume construction of the Fourth Avenue Theater in Anchorage. The architectural firm of C. Marcus Priteca and A.A. Porreca settled on an Art Deco design, which was fashionable in the early 1940s, for the 1,000 seat theater. The exterior of the theater was to have clean lines with a pattern of large squares in the cement in order to break up the expansive wall fronting on the street.[114] On May 29, 1947, the *Anchorage Daily Times* gave the following description of the interior:

> Touring the theater's ultra-gorgeous interior is like walking through a kaleidoscope.
>
> The basic color is warm rose with blue and chartreuse secondary shades lavishly high-lighted with gilt borders and decorations.
>
> The Alaskan flag twinkles in the blue ceiling when the house lights are on and glows dimly in the dark. Sky blue upholstery matches the ceiling.
>
> The heavy curtain, controlled by five motors, rises and drops in an interesting rhythmic action.
>
> The screen is framed in color and flanked by two

handsome murals by the Hineberg Decorating Co. of Los Angeles which were hauled over the Alaska highway in trucks last winter.

Hineberg experts worked here two months assembling the murals which show Yukon river boats, huskies, airplanes, the northern lights, gold- panning and other Alaskan scenery in gold-leaf.

Interior of 4th Avenue Theatre in Anchorage. *Photo courtesy of Anchorage Museum.*

A mural in the lobby shows Mount McKinley and the wall beside the stairway supports a gold-leaf collection of Alaskan animals (wolves, beavers, wild geese, squirrels, fish) and wild flowers.

A portrait of "Cap" Lathrop painted by Eustace Zeigler from a photograph, and presented as a surprise by Harry Hill, D.E. Hewitt, J.H. Clawson, Edward W. Coffey and E. Wells Ervin, hangs at the top of the stairs.

No patrons will be roped off and forgotten in the Fourth Avenue theater. One of the most attractive features is a beautifully fitted waiting room for 200. The room will be lined with couches and chairs. Standing lights will preclude eyestrain.

Lathrop took precautions to protect this interior. No provision was made for a concession stand and popcorn was to be forbidden within the theater.[115]

Mezzanine of 4th Avenue Theatre with Cap Lathrop's portrait. *Photo courtesy of Anchorage Museum.*

Crowds waiting to enter 4th Avenue Theatre on opening night. *Photo courtesy of Anchorage Museum.*

After an open house on Friday, the Fourth Avenue Theater officially opened on Saturday, May 31, 1947, with a showing of *The Jolson Story.*

Although Lathrop protested that he had nothing to say, he was called to the stage and remarked, "This is the happiest day of my life." After giving special credit to the builders, he commented: "When I saw the lineup in front of the Empress theater during the war, I said I would do something to repay the people of Anchorage for the grief they went through while I was trying to build. It took a long time to finish it, but I think we have something better than we started in 1941."[116]

Interior of 4th Avenue Theatre on opening night. L to R — E. Wells Ervin, Louis and Stella Odsather. Cap Lathrop is behind Mrs. Odsather; the man in uniform is Col. Thomas Mosley, commanding officer at Fort Richardson. *Photo courtesy of Anchorage Museum.*

The editor of the *Anchorage Daily Times* explained the difficulties:

> Construction of this modern building was marked by trouble. Started in 1941, the work had to be halted during the war. Materials were not available. Shipping space was insufficient to allow the movement of those materials that

were available. Labor conditions were such as to further complicate the picture.

During the years the building project was at a standstill, Capt. A.E. Lathrop, the owner, quietly made his construction program more elaborate. While friends sympathized with him for the delays, Lathrop was engaged in changing the original plans to make them more and more difficult to achieve and slower to complete. This policy was effected under conditions which would usually have resulted in a simplification and cheapening of the building project so as to speed completion. ...

The greatest significance is one that will touch the daily lives and thinking of all persons who call Alaska home. The Fourth Avenue theater is more than an expensive and elaborate building. It is a landmark in the development of a city in which families live, work, play and die. ...

Captain Lathrop, by investing his money in the Fourth Avenue theater, has shown his conviction that Anchorage has a brilliant future and his business is more than a 'boom' proposition. Other businessmen will adopt the same policy and great improvements in business and recreational facilities can be expected.

During the immediate post-war period, Lathrop also made a significant contribution to recreational facilities in Fairbanks. On June 21, 1946, he drove the first golf ball onto the golf course being developed on land near the KFAR transmitter station that he had donated for that purpose. The nine hole golf course, a joint project of the Rotary Club, the Chamber of Commerce, the Fairbanks Lions Club, and the Spring Carnival Association, was financed initially by selling $100 life memberships to 215 people. The clubhouse, completed in October, 1946, soon became the favorite social center and meeting place for large Fairbanks gatherings, including hearings before traveling Congressional committees.[117] General Dwight D. Eisenhower, an avid golfer, played the Fairbanks course in 1946 when only three holes were completed and returned the next summer to address more than 300 guests at the country club. In the course of his speech he paid special tribute to Lathrop:

... And here I should like to digress for a moment to do something I have never done before in a public gathering — and that is to single out and mention an individual present at that time. And I am not going to be coy — I am going to mention the name of the man who in Alaska, it seems to me, has lived more in the future, the man that I hear on all sides called 'Cap'. If he, many years ago, hadn't believed in the future of Alaska, it is perfectly clear that there are many conveniences of the daily life that you people live that you would not now enjoy. He lived for a future and he has worked for a future! So, as I pause to express one word of admiration for his life, I am not thinking so much of the success he has attained in the world of industry and of the remuneration he has received theretofore. I speak of the faith he has had in an idea and in a place, and it is in that sense we must look to our own country.[118]

POLITICS — 1946-1949
The New Deal Comes to Alaska

Although Alaskans still praised Cap Lathrop for his fore-sight in spearheading the development of Alaska, the political climate in post-war Alaska was changing. Returning veterans and new emigrants from the "States" were demanding a great-er voice in government of the Territory and the full rights of citizenship that statehood would bring. These new Alaskans protested against the power of lobbyists representing interests of absentee owners of fishing, mining and transportation en-terprises. Since Lathrop welcomed outside capital as essential for the development of Alaska and associated with powerful Seattle absentee owners, the new progressives began to ques-tion the motivation of Alaska's "homegrown millionaire."

Since a strong gold-mining industry had protected Alaska's economy from the effects of the depression of the 1930s, New Deal philosophy, emphasizing taxation to subsidize government construction and social programs, was slow to reach the Northern territory. Alaska's first Democratic gov-ernor during the Roosevelt administration, John W. Troy, a former Juneau newspaper editor, was not a committed New Dealer. When Troy resigned for health reasons in 1939, Presi-dent Roosevelt appointed Ernest Gruening, who had been the Director of Territories for the Interior Department, with the mandate to bring the New Deal to Alaska.[119]

Gruening, a well-to-do Harvard-educated liberal, was the antithesis of a self-made conservative like Cap Lathrop. The two men were destined to be political antagonists. In an in-terview for the *Alaska Weekly* back in 1935, Lathrop had giv-en the following assessment of the New Deal:

Money is being literally dumped out by the ton in an effort to build up a political machine to hold the vast army of nitwits who are running the country in office and keep them on the public payroll. There is not a branch of the government that is being operated on an economical or a common sense basis. That money that is being wasted will have to be paid back some time, and taxation is mounting until it will soon be nothing short of confiscation. Under the present system, they are destroying the incentive to build up a business or a property and unless we make a change and make it before it is too late, we are headed for the worst Communistic condition that Marx ever imagined.[120]

Although some conservative Democrats from Juneau and Nome protested the appointment of Gruening because he

was not a resident Alaskan, Lathrop's *Fairbanks Daily News-Miner* welcomed the new governor and expressed the hope that "between the new executive and the people of Alaska there will exist the utmost harmony and singleness of purpose that will crown his stewardship with success and bring to Alaska an enduring era of prosperity and progress."[121] When Gruening stated that his aims for Alaska included development of more industry and a greater popu-

Governor Ernest Gruening. *Photo courtesy of Anchorage Museum.*

lation, better airports and aids to navigation, more ships to facilitate the tourist surge, an international highway to connect Alaska with the States, and ultimate statehood for Alaska, the *News-Miner* agreed.[122] In stating these goals, Gruening made no mention of increased taxation, but when the Territorial legislature convened in January 1941, he presented a taxation bill, drawn up by Professor Albert Harsh of the University of Washington law school,[123] which included a two per cent personal net income tax, a four per cent corporate net income tax, and a flat rate of ten mills as a general property tax. The governor insisted that these taxes were necessary to finance increased territorial spending and the construction of new national guard armories.[124]

The chambers of commerce in Anchorage and Fairbanks promptly passed resolutions opposing any new taxation,[125] and the legislature turned down both the new taxes and the construction of armories.[126] Gruening countered by composing a lengthy "Message to the People of Alaska" in which he condemned the legislature for rejecting his program and blamed the defeat on the influence of lobbyists representing absentee owners. "The underlying issue", he concluded, "is whether the absentees who are stripping, and would continue to strip, Alaska, shall through their resident lobbyists and representatives take it all. Or, whether the people of Alaska shall take their part and plow it back for the improvement and welfare of the Territory which they call their home."[126]

Most of the Alaska newspapers published Gruening's message, but the *Fairbanks Daily News-Miner* ignored it, an omission for which Gruening blamed Cap Lathrop.[127] During this pre-war period, Gruening was acutely aware of the antipathy that old-timers had for newcomers to Alaska.[128] The ambitious New Dealer may have envied the popularity of the soft-spoken, silver-haired Fairbanks tycoon. Lathrop was not alone in his opposition to Gruening's legislative program. In an editorial accompanying the first installment of Gruening's message, the *Anchorage Daily Times* commented:

> While this newspaper disagrees with the governor in most of his statements and especially in his principal conclusion — that the gold and cannery lobbies dominated the legislature — it is a pleasure to present his views for the consideration of the people of Alaska.

The governor was defeated at almost every turn in his

legislative program. His pet bill — that provided for the construction of armories in Alaska — was among those that failed to pass. Never before has an Alaskan governor been handed such a stiff and sweeping rebuke as that given by the past session. ...

The governor apparently was desirous of stating his case and has turned to the newspapers as the medium. ... We reserve the right, however, to disagree editorially with his views. To us it appears that the governor — a defeated appointee of the Ickes crowd — is making a plea to the people who refused to accept his leadership. There is an indication in the message that it may be a 'declaration of war,' as the governor seems to be intent on continuing his battle for the next two years and once more attempting to saddle Alaska with new taxes and an expanding territorial government.

In his opening statement, the governor sets forth that the basic issue confronting Alaska is whether the territory shall be run by lobbyists. He declares the lobbyists made a sweeping victory in the past session and that the bills fostered by the governor were defeated by the lobby.

The governor points out in his message that 'things are not always what they seem.' It appears that there is 'the reality' in the situation as to the lobbyists. The chief lobbyist of the session appears to have been Governor Gruening himself and if half the accounts of the legislature are accurate, he conducted one of the most vigorous, extensive, and various lobbying campaigns ever witnessed at the foot of Mount Roberts.

Instead of the lobbyists dominating the legislature, it appears that the best interests of Alaska were in the driver's seat and 'the lobbyist' was defeated.[130]

Governor Gruening did not immediately continue his battle to "saddle Alaska with new taxes" because World War II intervened and all Alaskans, including the governor, were preoccupied with the war, some of which was fought on Alaska's own Aleutian islands. Alaskans did not voice any opposition to Gruening's appointment to a second term in 1944, and he was still governor when Alaska emerged from the war in 1946.

The battle resumed during a special session of the territorial legislature in 1946. The governor called for this session to consider special legislation to provide bonuses and services for returning veterans, and proposed to finance the veterans' programs with taxes similar to the ones he had introduced in 1941. The legislature agreed to provide for the veterans, but the Senate and the House of Representatives differed on a form of taxation to support the programs. In the end the Senate prevailed, and a sales tax, rather than an income tax, was enacted. During this special session Senator Norman Walker introduced a memorial which asked that "Governor Gruening be removed for political activities which are disrupting the Territory." The more progressive House retaliated with Representative Stanley McCutcheon's resolution lauding Gruening as "the greatest governor in the history of the Territory."[131]

The 1946 special legislative session did approve a measure to place a referendum on statehood on the ballot at the general election the following fall. In an interview immediately preceding the October 8th election, Lathrop expressed his reservations on the statehood issue:

I certainly hope Alaska eventually will become a state, but I sincerely do not believe now is the time to take this very important step.

The costs of setting up the machinery for statehood — such as the construction of necessary public buildings — would throw a terrific financial burden on a very small group of taxpayers. …

Immediately ahead for Alaska should be a period of great development of resources and transportation, scientific farming, establishment of a Southeastern Alaska pulp industry, and further steps in the fishing, mining and fur industries are expected. A railroad north from Prince George, B.C., should come before many years.

But Alaskans themselves do not have enough money for this large scale development. We must look to Outside capital to assist in the development.

It is only common sense to realize that financial interests contemplating investment in the Territory will think twice if confronted with the possibility of heavy, almost confiscatory taxes which must be levied on a small group of people to carry the cost of establishing and maintaining statehood.[132]

The referendum on immediate statehood for Alaska passed by a three-to-two margin throughout the Territory, while failing in the Nome and Fairbanks districts.[133] Passage of the statehood referendum was acknowledged to be a victory for Gruening, however the legislators elected to serve in the upcoming Eighteenth Territorial Legislative session were still unwilling to accept many of the governor's proposals. The Senate again killed the income tax bill supported by the governor.[134] When Robert B. Atwood, the editor of the *Anchorage Daily Times* arrived in Juneau to observe the final days of the session, he observed that "almost everyone is mad at everyone and conflicting opinions mark the reasoning behind the mad." He further elaborated on the basis for the discontent:

> Outstanding, as usual, is the long-established feud between the pro- and anti-governor forces. ...
> We are advised that the desire to embarrass, harass, and ham-string the governor is so keen nothing else matters in the minds of some legislators. ...
> Another interesting study, available for the newcomer without any extensive research is the influence of the canned salmon lobby. W.C. Arnold, counsel for the salmon industry and eminent in Alaska as the lobbyist at all legislative sessions, is commonly referred to among legislators as well as spectators as 'Senator' Arnold.[136]

After the Eighteenth Territorial Legislature adjourned in April 1947, Governor Gruening issued another "Governor's Message", in which he again criticized the legislature for "failure to enact basic tax legislation." He further pointed out that, because of poor mining and fishing seasons, the usual taxes on these industries would be insufficient to cover the appropriations made by the legislature.[136]

National magazines were beginning to take notice of Gruening's efforts to combat apathy and vested interests in

Alaska. The June 16, 1947, issue of *Time* featured Gruening's picture on the cover and a four-page article explaining how Alaska's governor had "gone on the warpath" against absentee industry that was gutting the Territory, and was arguing for statehood and the "abolition of his own job."

Alaska received additional publicity later that summer when the House Sub-committee on Territories and Insular Possessions held hearings in Alaska. At Anchorage, the focal point of the statehood movement, all of the testimony during the August 30 and 31 hearings favored statehood.[137] Testimony in Fairbanks was mixed with some opponents expressing doubts that Alaska could support the additional costs of statehood. Lathrop did not testify at these hearings, but a *Fairbanks Daily News-Miner* editorial stated that "like most Alaskans, we are FOR STATEHOOD — BUT NOT STATEHOOD NOW." The editorial also pointed out that statehood would not be a "cure- all for everything from transportation tie-ups to the alleged foibles of our Territorial legislatures." The *News-Miner* reprinted an editorial from Juneau's *Daily Alaska Empire* expressing doubts that a published economic report by Gruening's friend, George Sundberg, had given the voters a true picture of the potential costs of statehood.[138]

While pro- and anti-statehood factions were arguing about whether Alaska could afford statehood, the Territory was having difficulty meeting its financial obligations. Governor Gruening arrived in Fairbanks on January 9, 1948, to discuss means by which to prevent closure of the University of Alaska. The governor expressed reluctance to call for a special session of the legislature until a new group of lawmakers could be elected. In an address at the Empress Theater the governor revealed that the president of Alaska Airlines had offered a $25,000 interest-free loan to tide the University over, and that Captain Lathrop, a member of the board of regents, had assured him that private businesses would provide the $200,000 necessary to keep the university from closing.[139] Lathrop then pledged a $25,000 interest-free loan himself and wrote letters appealing to other Alaska businesses.[140]

Lathrop cooperated with Gruening in keeping the university from closing. However, when President Truman nominated Gruening to serve another four-year term as governor of Alaska, Lathrop promptly registered his opposition. In a signed editorial on the front page of the *Fairbanks Daily News-Miner*, he insisted that "there are many other compelling reasons — outside the realm of partisan politics — which should give the Senators pause in their consideration of the Gruening nomination." He went on to describe the governor's attempts to pass tax measures that were not acceptable to the legislators and concluded:

> The plain explanation is that the governor has insisted on HIS program and no other. ... The people of Alaska now find themselves caught in a stalemate between Gruening and the lawmakers who refuse him the unquestioning obedience which he demands. ...
>
> The conclusion is inescapable that Gruening has tried to use the power and prestige of his office and the resources of the federal government to transfer to himself the initiative and law-making powers of the citizens. It is the hallmark of all New Dealers. ...
>
> There can be no doubt that his demands for steadily increasing taxes on enterprises already in the Territory and his attempts to stir the people against 'absentee' owners have had their costly effect in discouraging the risking of new capital in Alaska. ...
>
> Alaska, if it is to grow, must have new capital and new enterprise. It must have a governor who has the foresight to appreciate this necessity and who is able to inspire the confidence that will draw the added commerce to the Territory. Gruening has made an issue of Statehood for Alaska. Like most Alaskans, we are for statehood at the proper time. But we recognize that statehood will not provide an automatic cure-all for all the Territory's ills.
>
> We believe that before we consider assuming the tremendous responsibility and financial burden which statehood will entail, we must set our Territorial house in order.
>
> As the first move in so doing, we suggest that the Senate Committee on Interior and Insular Affairs reject without undue delay President Truman's nomination of Ernest Gruening for another term as governor of Alaska.[141]

The battle lines were drawn. In Fairbanks, a bitter campaign prior to the April 27 primary election was climaxed when two university students, running for state representative as Democrats, accused Lathrop of trying to make President Bunnell interfere with their political activity. The allegations were promptly denied by both Lathrop and Bunnell, and the students lost in the primary.[142]

In Anchorage, Harry J. Hill, a Lathrop associate and president of the Northern Publishing Company, sought to neutralize the pro-statehood stand of the *Anchorage Daily Times* by helping Norman Brown's weekly *Anchorage News* become a daily publication. On May 3, 1948, the day that radio station KENI started broadcasting in Anchorage, the first issue of the *Anchorage Daily News* rolled off the presses.[143]

Lathrop had for years considered buying an Anchorage newspaper. Shortly after Robert Atwood bought the *Anchorage Daily Times* in 1935, Lathrop presented him the ultimatum, "either you sell me the paper or I'll run you out of town." Cap evidently suspected that Atwood, the son-in-law of Edward A. Rasmuson, would make the *Times* a mouthpiece for the opposing faction of the Republican party. The two men could not agree on a price, so Lathrop frequently pointed to the Fourth Avenue Theater lot as the future site for the Anchorage paper he planned to establish.[144] The *Anchorage Daily News* editor repeatedly denied that Cap Lathrop dictated editorial policy,[145] but on statehood matters the *Anchorage Daily News* and the *Fairbanks Daily News-Miner* usually agreed.

Congress postponed definitive action on the Gruening nomination and the Alaska and Hawaii statehood bills until after the November election. Although a Republican victory was anticipated, Truman was elected and his choice of Gruening for another term as Alaska's governor remained to be confirmed. In Alaska, the voters registered their dissatisfaction about the financial problems of the Territory by defeating many of the incumbent legislators. Governor Gruening took advantage of the situation by calling for a special session of the legislature to consider the tax program.[146] Recognizing that "the new legislature appears to be dominated by the so- called progressives who are in accord with the governor's tax program," the editor of the *Anchorage Daily Times* urged caution:

> It appears that an income tax will be enacted for the first time. Among other taxes proposed are those on property, business licenses and retail sales. The latter seems to have the least support among the legislators.
>
> If the legislature enacts such a program, it must be expected that the complaints of Alaskans will undergo a sudden change. Instead of grumbling about the failures of the last legislature, the complaints will be focused on the new legislature and the 'oppressive' tax program it enacts.
>
> If the legislature attempts to correct in one year all the ailments of the past 10 years, the impact on businesses and individuals will be substantial. ...
>
> Thus temperance in legislative action might be the main problem — a temperance that will result in sufficient new revenue to finance territorial obligations and not run beyond the realm of reasonableness or what the taxpayers are in a position to take.[147]

Legislators at the special session immediately passed laws levying a net income tax, and, by the end of the regular session, they had enacted other revenue reforms, including a uniform business-license tax, a tobacco tax, an augmented fish-trap-license tax, raw-fish taxes, and increased fisherman's-license taxes.[148] Gruening was elated, and his subsequent "Message to the People of Alaska" summarizing the performance of the nineteeth legislature was filled with unqualified praise.[149]

While Gruening was enjoying success in Juneau, some of his opponents were protesting his confirmation, and the Senate Interior Committee voted unanimously to postpone action pending public hearings in Washington, D.C.[150] On March 30, 1949, two groups of Alaskans crowded the hearing chambers — seven opponents of the Gruening nomination, led by Austin E. Lathrop and A.H. Zeigler of Ketchikan, and a delegation of 44 Gruening supporters, who arrived on a special plane chartered by Representative Stanley McCutcheon. In the course of his testimony Lathrop characterized Gruening as a dictator, stating:

> Gruening doesn't belong in Alaska at all. His interest

is in personal promotion of Gruening rather than interest in the territory.

He has been pitting one element of Alaska against another, screaming for development on one side of his mouth and proposing prohibitive taxes on the other. He attacks absentee ownership on one hand and invites the pulp industry into Alaska on the other. Yet the pulp mills would be absentee owned. What would Alaska be without outside capital?[151]

In the end, Lathrop tempered his criticism by saying, "Governor Gruening... is in my view a fine man. I like him in many respects. I like him because I get ideas from him."[152] Charles D. Jones, a Territorial senator from Nome, injected humor into the hearings by discarding his written testimony, which had been edited by Lathrop's secretary to read, "when all else fails, he (Gruening) plies them with cocktails and cultured conversation," and explained in his own words that, "he fills 'em full of booze and gives 'em lots of conversation." Jones then went on to elaborate: "Let me tell you brother. The way he is throwing it out, you know, we have an expression, that what he peddles makes the grass grow green on the Kougarok. He's got it. Dairy farmers know what it is."[153] The Gruening supporters testified briefly, describing Gruening in such unqualified glowing terms that even Alaska's Delegate Bob Bartlett, a staunch Gruening supporter, was sickened.[154] In his lengthy testimony at the end of the hearings, Gruening singled out Lathrop as the owner of numerous enterprises in Alaska that were not paying there fair share of taxes.[155]

Since the testimony at the hearings failed to substantiate any dishonesty or malfeasance during Gruening's two term as Alaska's governor, he was quickly confirmed for the third term.[156] Cap Lathrop had lost his battle with the New Deal.

DEATH AND TAXATION — 1950
Statehood Drive Continues

During the hearings on Gruening's confirmation for a third term, Cap Lathrop stated that he was suspending future building plans because of the governor's tax programs.[157] He did not mention what the plans were, but he still had a building to finish in Anchorage — a transmission facility for KENI, the sister station for KFAR. Although KENI began broadcasting in May 1948, the station was occupying temporary quarters in the Fourth Avenue theater building. As in his previous buildings, Lathrop spared no expense in designing and constructing the 30-by-72-foot reinforced concrete building on the south bank of Chester Creek. In addition to the control rooms and maintenance shop, the building contained walnut-paneled living quarters for the engineering staff.[158]

KENI Transmitter building in Anchorage.

Lathrop was in Anchorage on July 10, 1949, to dedicate the transmitter station and also new offices and studios on the third floor of the Fourth Avenue theater building. Cap continued to concentrate on radio and filed applications for additional new radio stations in Juneau and Ketchikan.[159] He resisted the desire of associates to start television because he feared it might cut in on the patronage of his theaters.[160] Lathrop had difficulty adjusting to other modern developments. He objected to airmail delivery in rural Alaska because he felt it would not give storekeepers time to sell their goods before being billed for them. In his early days in the transfer business, Lathrop frequently postponed billing for delivery until goods could be sold. J.B. Gottstein, pioneer wholesale grocer, once related that he got a good start in Anchorage in 1915 because Cap Lathrop allowed him to sell a load of cigars before charging for their delivery.[161]

In politics, as well, the octogenarian entrepreneur was behind the times. More young people were moving to Alaska and joining the statehood movement, orchestrated by Governor Gruening. When the Alaska statehood bill passed in the House of Representatives on March 3, 1950, by a vote of 186 to 146, Gruening stated that the vote was "most gratifying", while Lathrop, interviewed in Seattle on his way back from Washington, D.C., where he attended a meeting of the Republican National Policy Committee, expressed surprise at the size of the opposition. "Nobody in the House could hurt himself by voting for it, since the Senate is there to make sure the bill will go no further," he explained. "The State of Alaska would send one Representative and two Senators to Washington. Four hundred thirty-five Representatives don't worry too much about one more member, but 96 Senators will think a moment before they consent to two more."[162]

In the meantime, Gruening continued to single Lathrop out as his enemy. At a Jefferson-Jackson dinner in Fairbanks the day after the House statehood vote, he lashed out against William C. Strand, the editor of the *Fairbanks Daily News-Miner*, describing him as "a newspaperman whom `Cap' Lathrop brought in not long ago to pep up the paper, propagate his ideas, carry out his policies, fight statehood, prevent the present governor from getting reappointed and, if reappointed, to prevent his confirmation; and to build up the Republican party generally, or at least the right wing of the party."[163]

The long-standing division within the Republican party appeared to be ending following the death of National Committeeman E.A. Rasmuson the previous year, and the Republicans held their first united caucus in 16 years at Juneau on March 30, 1950. As a plank in its platform, the Party reaffirmed its stand on the need for Alaskan statehood, but attacked the current HR 331 as inadequate "in that it fails to specify the respective rights and privileges and the respective duties and obligations of the federal government and the proposed State of Alaska." On the final day, the caucus unanimously elected Austin E. Lathrop to replace Rasmuson. In nominating him, the Republican national committeewoman referred to Lathrop as "one who has the respect of the people that he has come into contact with; one who has integrity; one who has principle and one who has invested in his home, the Territory of Alaska."

In accepting the position, Lathrop said, in part: "I cannot refrain from letting you know the inspiring and welcome sight of this united Republican party of Alaska. It goes without saying that I feel very proud to have been given this high honor and I want you to know that I am deeply grateful. I did not seek this honor. As most of you know my own affairs keep me very busy, and now Governor Gruening proposes to assist me."[164]

This reference to Gruening undoubtedly referred to the recent naming of Lathrop and his Healy River Coal Corporation, along with Usibelli Coal Company and the Evan Jones Coal Company, as defendants in a Sherman anti-trust probe for alleged agreement to allocate and divide the market for hard fuel in Alaska and for fixing the price of coal supplied to military installations in Alaska. Other defendants in the antitrust probes included the Alaska Steamship Company and some liquor distributors, dry cleaners and cab companies.[165] Gilbert W. Skinner, president of Alaska Steamship Company, openly accused Gruening, terming the suits "the latest attempt to harass and embarrass the Alaska Steamship Company and to make way for socialized government operation of steamship service to the territory." "The alleged charges and the Justice Department inquiries have been instigated and sponsored by Governor Gruening," he declared. "We have been so informed by representatives of the Department of Justice and others. This indictment is our penalty for my refusal to make a 'deal' on the Alaska statehood issue."[166] Gruening denied the charges, and the *Daily Alaska Empire* editor in Juneau commented:

Anyone who is even faintly familiar with the manner in which the present administration plays its game of politics will take with the usual grain of salt Governor Gruening's statement that, as far as the grand jury proceedings in Anchorage are concerned, he knows 'only what I read in the papers.'

From the moment the first subpoenas in the 'anti-trust' cases were issued, indications have been that it was all a political scheme to punish certain people who did not go along with the administration's plans for statehood, for Territorial liquor control, or for more taxes on fisheries. ...

Whether the fight against Captain Lathrop is because he is an important political figure in the Territory who, with a forthright honesty, has opposed statehood for Alaska because he can see no way for the taxpayers of the Territory to carry the costs of statehood, we don't know.

We do know that back in 1941, Captain Lathrop, together with other prominent anti-administration persons were subject to investigation for alleged lobbying during the 1941 session of the legislature — an investigation instigated, there is little doubt, by Gov. Gruening. And Capt. Lathrop, who has put every penny he has made in the Territory back into business to further develop Alaska, is now a principal in the trust-busting cases.

We do not know that the Anchorage indictments are the result of a planned political persecution, but we do know that they fit into the pattern of reprisals that we in Alaska have come to expect — and to fear.

Nearly ten years ago a prominent Democrat, after fighting through the 1941 legislature with Gov. Gruening said this: 'The only trouble with the Governor is that you can be 99 per cent for him and one per cent against him — and he will be 100 per cent against you.'

There are a lot of people who are paying for being 1 per cent against Gov. Gruening, whose modesty as regards his influence cannot be taken too seriously.[167]

Lathrop did not testify at the Senate Statehood hearings in April 1950. The main anti-statehood witness, W.C. Arnold, complained that HR 331 would make Alaska a "pauper state" because it did not provide adequate land for the new state.[168] Although this may have been primarily a delaying tactic of the canned salmon industry, the Senate committee did decide to revise the bill to give more land to the prospective state.

While awaiting further action on both the statehood bill and the anti-trust investigation, Lathrop won praise from the *Anchorage Daily Times* for the same type of civic conscious- ness that he had frequently displayed through the years in Anchorage, Fairbanks and Cordova:

> It is an event worthy of more than casual notice when a business establishment suspends its regular operations voluntarily and turns over its facilities for the free use of a community project. ...
>
> School officials discovered that the high school audito- rium, which has been used for commencement programs for many years, was far from adequate for the 1950 cer- emonies. ...
>
> Cap Lathrop solved the problem when he ordered the shows cancelled for the day so that his Fourth Avenue theater could be used.
>
> He made it possible for the Anchorage graduates to enjoy a memorable commencement program which will always be a milestone in their lives.[169]

Early in July defense lawyers filed several motions in the anti-trust case against the Healy River Coal Corporation and the Third District court announced that arraignment of the case would take place on August 29. When interviewed by an edi- tor of the Portland *Oregonian*, Lathrop denied that the three named coal companies had ever discussed prices. He further asserted that they "sure as hell haven't divided the market — nature and circumstances did a good job of that." The Healy River coal, he explained, was sub-bituminous and not appro- priate for use in trains, while the Evan Jones coal was wet and would freeze if shipped to Fairbanks, where he had built coal storage bunkers to protect the Healy River coal.[170]

Lathrop was not destined to see the outcome of the antitrust case. Soon after this interview he boarded an Alaska Railroad train for the Healy River mine, where he spent the morning of July 26, 1950, supervising a crew repairing the approach to the Coal Creek bridge. After lunch he left to return alone to the rail yards and was found lying beside the tracks a few moments later by the mine timekeeper. No one actually observed the accident, but he apparently was killed instantly when run over by a loaded coal car.[171]

Healy River coal mine in 1952. *Photo courtesy of Anchorage Museum.*

The following words, spoken by A. Leslie Nerland at Memorial Services in the Fairbanks Empress Theatre, are representative of the many editorials and eulogies that filled newspapers in Alaska and the Pacific Northwest:

> There is no need here today to enumerate the material achievements of Austin E. Lathrop. They are too well known and too obvious to even a stranger in Alaska to need recounting. They stand, and will stand for years, as monuments to his memory; and more important, will serve as an inspiration to younger generations to build Alaska well, and to build it permanently. There is no way of knowing how many of our present citizens in Alaska have reached their success because of Cap's contagious

faith and belief in the Territory. He has led the way. He has pointed the direction to the goal. The course is plotted for those who follow him. ... Cap Lathrop will be remembered as a man of tremendous capacities, both in vision and for work. The epoch of his years in Alaska marked the transition from the frontier stage to the development of modern buildings designed to endure permanently. He was the one man, more than anyone else, who ushered in the Alaska of today and the future. He was a man of strong will and virtually limitless imagination, which was unaffected by the passage of the years or his own increasing age. In the direction of his enterprises and the steady expansion of his interests, he demonstrated a marvelous capacity for keeping abreast of the times spanned by his long life. He was a man who played little and who worked hard and long. ...

Cap was never blessed with a family in the everyday sense of the word. The only family recognized in the years that we have known him, was much greater in number than any usual family could be. Because here in Fairbanks, in Anchorage, in Cordova, in Suntrana and other places in Alaska, he looked upon the members of his organization as part of his responsibility. Cap knew how to be a stern father, but those who understood, conceded that he knew best; and almost without fail his good judgment was confirmed by the passage of time. When one of Cap's people became troubled, there was never a more sympathetic listener or more willing assistance. And, outside of his interests, so many of you here today know within your hearts the extent of his quiet charity that came without hesitation for his old-time friends and the institutions of Alaska.[172]

Following the local memorial services, Lathrop's body was flown to Seattle where funeral services were held at the First Methodist Church, followed by burial in the Lathrop family plot in Forest Lawn cemetery alongside his parents and two sisters. Lathrop remembered both his natural family and his extended Alaskan family of employees and friends with generous bequests of stock in the Lathrop company. He also left stock to hospitals in Anchorage and Fairbanks; cash bequests to be divided among Catholic and Protestant churches in Anchorage, Fairbanks and Cordova; an endowment for scholarships to the University of Alaska; and cash bequests to over a hundred employees varying from $500 to $800 depending on length of service. Lathrop's nephew, Austin Cooley; his secretary, Miriam Dickey; his lawyer, Edward F. Medley; and business associates, Harry J. Hill, Sydney C. Raynor and L.W. Baker, were named as trustees of the "Lathrop Trust" which would operate the Lathrop interests for five years. The Lathrop estate was valued conservatively as "in excess of $500,000", but outside sources estimated it might actually be worth three to four million dollars.[173]

END OF AN EMPIRE — 1951-1958
Ice Palace and Statehood

The trustees continued to operate the diverse Lathrop enterprises for five years as prescribed in Cap's will. Then some businesses split off and were purchased by their former managers. Alvin Bramstedt bought the radio stations and pioneered successfully in the television field, as did the engineer, August Hiebert. Sydney Raynor was not as fortunate. The Cordova Empress Theatre and apartment building burned shortly after he purchased them.

The Healy River Coal company also suffered reverses as a result of labor disputes and underground fires, and lost its position as Alaska's foremost coal producer. The anti-trust case dragged on until November 1951 when a Fairbanks jury convicted the Healy River company.[174] Since jury members acquitted the other defendants, they evidently felt that Lathrop had been guilty of colluding with himself to fix coal prices. Testimony in the case centered around the allegation of a former Healy River employee that a meeting of coal operators had occurred at which prices were discussed. A defense witness denied any agreements were reached at the meeting.[175]

The Lathrop will provided that William Strand should have six months in which to decide whether he wished to purchase the *Fairbanks Daily News Miner*. Since he did not exercise this option, the newspaper was purchased by C.W. Sneeden, who continued supporting Republican candidates but eventually altered the paper's anti-statehood stand.[176]

Although pro-statehood sentiment continued to grow in Alaska, the Senate balked at adding additional members from Hawaii and Alaska, much as Lathrop had predicted. When the nation elected a Republican president, Dwight D. Eisenhower, in 1952, Gruening was replaced as Alaska's governor by Frank Heinzelman, who openly opposed statehood.[177] Gruening, however, persevered in his fight for statehood and was elected a nominal senator-elect under the Tennessee plan adopted by Alaska's Constitutional Convention in 1955. In this capacity, Gruening and his compatriots, William Egan and Ralph Rivers traveled to Washington to lobby for statehood. Realizing that nationwide publicity would help in the fight, Gruening persuaded an old acquaintance, popular novelist Edna Ferber, to write a book on Alaska that would promote the statehood cause.[178] Ferber, who had recently won wide acclaim for *Giant*, her book on Texas, made several trips to Alaska, where she was enthusiastically received by statehood advocates. At Gruening's request *Anchorage Daily Times* editor Robert Atwood and his wife helped Miss Ferber meet people during these trips. Atwood's recollections of the man who threatened to run him out of town may have influenced the author in her choice of Cap Lathrop as the prototype for Czar Kennedy, the statehood antagonist in her book.

Before finishing the novel, Miss Ferber was stricken with a painful illness and barely managed to rush it through to meet her deadline.[179] Late in the spring of 1958 Gruening reviewed the galley proofs for the Ferber novel, and on May 27, the day that Congressional hearings on Alaska statehood were scheduled to begin, *Ice Palace* arrived on bookstands throughout the nation.

A brief synopsis of *Ice Palace* states: "There are the two titans of the older generation, whose fifty-year battle to decide whether the exploiters or the builders will rule Alaska, is about to reach a climax." Although the author proclaimed that "no character in this book is meant as a portrayal of a real person", Alaskan residents had no difficulty identifying the exploiter, Czar Kennedy, with Cap Lathrop, Gruening's old enemy. The following Kennedy enterprises in "Baranof" were similar to Lathrop's in Fairbanks:

...The *Ice Palace*. They loved it, they bragged about it. Czar Kennedy had built it as he had built most of the town's show places. On the corner of Gold and Polaris was the Miners' National Bank, Czar Kennedy, Presi-

115

dent; just across the street the Kennedy Block housed the town's largest motion-picture theater; a drugstore dispensed everything from tuna sandwiches to television sets; a hardware store; a supermarket. Solidly situated halfway down the street stood the three- story printing plant and editorial offices of the Baranof *Daily Lode*. Czar Kennedy, President and Publisher, the masthead read."

Czar Kennedy also owned a coal mine, and he, like Lathrop, died there in an accident at the end of the book. The following descriptions of Czar Kennedy are undeniably word portraits of Cap Lathrop:

But Czar Kennedy — there was a man they could understand. A picturesque and romantic figure from youth to old age, he had a quiet word and a smile for everyone. To look at him, Baranof boasted, you'd think he didn't have one penny to rub against another. In appearance a composite of philosopher, fresh-water college professor, with, perhaps, just a touch of Mississippi River gambler. From this mixture he emerged handsome, approachable, benign, somewhat scholarly. He never read a book.

Waylaid by one of his nostalgic contemporaries, Czar Kennedy had schooled himself to the appearance of interested listener. Politic, suave, it was his business to keep the Territory quiescent, uninformed. His head a little to one side in the attitude of listening, the battered hat pushed back on the luxuriant wavy white hair, the fine eyes gently humorous and understanding, he would occasionally nod his head in agreement and utter a low wordless hum of appreciation. The professional charmer, the shrewd operator, he heard practically nothing that the garrulous oldster was saying, and cared less.

These last remarks scarcely do justice to a man who visited old timers in the Fairbanks hospital almost every day and spent hours talking with them about old times.[180] Other characterizations of Czar Kennedy were less complementary:

To Czar Kennedy ... the Territory was pure plunder,

rich, bountiful, inexhaustible. To Thor Storm, the gentle giant of the scholarly scientific mind, ... Alaska was a place of blinding beauty and endless promise, a possible example of hope in a frantic world, if only it could be saved from the ravishment of predatory men like Czar.

Thor Storm, Ferber's hero, tells Kennedy what he thinks of him in several passages:

What a snob you are, Czar! You build banks and movie houses and high buildings. You pretend to be plain and simple. You love power and position. Perhaps it might have been better for the Territory — and for you — if you had done so. (gotten married) You've compensated, they call it in the new language — you've taken out your natural human urges in a passion for power. Power passion. Many men do that. It doesn't work out too well. Hitler —

Alaskan greeted *Ice Palace* with reservations, realizing that it was not as good a story as *Giant* or other earlier Ferber novels. The editor of the *Anchorage Daily Times* observed:

Literary experts may debate the merits of the novel for years, but there is no question that Miss Ferber has rendered a valuable service to Alaska by writing it.

Anything she writes becomes a best seller and Alaska will benefit from the wide readership her newest novel is bound to have. Her story, basically correct in facts, will go far in winning the understanding of Alaska that has long been lacking.

This has already been recognized by Outside book reviewers. *The New York Times* review said:

'Edna Ferber, the John Gunther of our novelists, has advanced her campaigning field from Texas to Alaska. In her new book *Ice Palace*, she has a territory twice the size of Texas to Guntherize. She makes the most of it with unflagging zeal among the mountains, the snows, and the seals. Her story is too repetitious and disorderly to win a prize in the world of literature. But I shouldn't be surprised at all to hear that it had helped measurable to win statehood for Alaska.'[181]

Lulu Fairbanks, Cap Lathrop and Eva McGown in 1939. Bridie Ballintyne in *Ice Palace* was said to have been inspired by Eva McGown.

Soon after *Ice Palace* was published Alaska did finally win statehood. Gruening, in his autobiography, *Many Battles*, speaks with pride about his role in promoting the novel:

> My friendship with Edna Ferber had begun years earlier... Having been an admirer of her fiction, I suggested

that she write a novel about Alaska and told her of our problems and our desire for statehood. She became interested, and made several trips to Alaska for background. The novel, *Ice Palace*, made a strong case for statehood. While some literary critics felt that it was not up to her best work, one of them, Clifton Fadiman, referred to it correctly as "the Uncle Tom's Cabin for Alaska," and that useful label gained currency. Thousands who might not have been interested in nonfiction accounts about Alaska did read her novel, and in the spring of 1958 the book stimulated many pro- statehood letters to members of Congress. They came at just the right time.[182]

The thousands of readers who espoused the cause of Alaska statehood may also have come to identify Cap Lathrop with Czar Kennedy, a plunderer rather than a builder of Alaska. The motion picture based on *Ice Palace*, which featured Richard Burton as Czar, further deviated from the Lathrop story.

Over half a century has passed since Captain Austin E. Lathrop died at the Healy River coal mine. A few Alaskans still alive who knew Cap personally remember him fondly; those that arrived during the post-war fight for statehood identify him with Czar Kennedy; and most newer Alaskans have no idea who Lathrop High School in Fairbanks is named for. The concrete foundations and walls of many of Lathrop's buildings are still standing although their facades and functions have changed. The Fourth Avenue Theater in Anchorage, the Lacey Street Theater in Fairbanks, and the KENI transmitter building still exist in the form in which they were built, and have been designated as historic buildings. Large motion picture theaters are no longer the social centers of Alaska's cities, but people interested in history hope that the Lathrop theaters can be preserved as examples of an era in Alaska's development and tributes to one of Alaska's first builders.

ENDNOTES

1. Della Banks. "A Game of Bluff". *Alaska Sportsman*, Oct. 1945.
2. A.W. Morgan. "Memories of Old Sunrise". Unpublished manuscript.
3. Della Banks. "Hope Springs Eternal". *Alaska Sportsman*, Jan. 1946.
4. "Report of Capt. Glenn". *Explorations in the Territory of Alaska*.
5. *Alaska Sportsman*, Feb. 1968, p.17.
6. *The Alaska Prospector*, May 8, 1902.
7. Ibid., October 1903.
8. John Koman. *Alaska's Turnagain Arm*, p.86.
9. Joan Alita Ray. "Cap Lathrop". *Alaskana*, Dec. 1971.
10. U.S.G.S. Bulletin #719, p.65.
11. A. Cameron Edwardson. "Eskimos Mined It —Russians Ignored It". *Alaska Industry*, Oct. 1969, pp.53-5.
12. Ibid.
13. *The Valdez News*, August 19, 1905.
14. *Cordova Alaskan*, October 6, 1906.
15. *Cordova Daily Alaskan*, December 19, 1908.
16. Hearst. "Alaska Midas". *Chicago Tribune Grafic Magazine*, Aug.8, 1948.
17. *Cordova Daily Alaskan*, June 14, 1910.
18. Ibid., December 9, 1909.
19. Miriam Dickey Kinsey. Unpublished manuscript.
20. "Cordova Coal Party". *Alaskana*, April 1947, p.18.
21. Ibid.
22. *Cordova Daily Alaskan*, December 3, 1912.
23. Ibid., August 31, 1912.
24. Ibid., June 18, 1912.
25. Ibid., April 24, 1914.
26. Ibid., February 24, 1912.
27. Ibid., June 25, 1914.
28. Ibid., January 7, 1913.
29. Ibid., June 25, 1914.
30. *Seward Gateway*, October 14, 1915.
31. *Anchorage Daily Times*, September 8, 1916.
32. Ibid., May 8, 1920.
33. Ibid., June 11, 1917.
34. Ibid., June 20, 1916.
35. Ibid., March 9, 1925.
36. Ibid., September 12, 1917.
37. Ibid., September 20, 1918.
38. *Cordova Daily Times,* November 22, 1919.

39. Ibid., February 28, 1920.
40. *Anchorage Daily Times*, November 3, 1920.
41. Ibid., March 28, 1921.
42. Ibid., May 14, 1921.
43. *Cordova Daily Times*, April 18, 1922.
44. *Anchorage Daily Times*, November 27, 1920.
45. *Cordova Daily Times*, March 29, 1922.
46. Ibid., July 31, 1922.
47. *Anchorage Daily Times*, August 28, 1922.
48. Ibid., March 16, 1923.
49. Ibid., March 23, 1923.
50. Ibid., April 9, 1923.
51. *The Alaska Weekly*, April 27, 1923.
52. Ibid., June 1, 1923. 53. Ibid., September 28, 1923.
54. *Anchorage Daily Times*, July 11, 1923.
55. Ibid., April 23, 1924.
56. *Cordova Daily Times*, August 14, 1923.
57. *Anchorage Daily Times*, July 21, 1923.
58. Ibid., December 11, 1923.
59. *Cordova Daily Times*, December 20, 1923.
60. *Anchorage Daily Times*, April 1, 1924.
61. *The New York Times Film Reviews*, May 13, 1924, 24:1.
62. *The Alaska Weekly*, May 20, 1924.
63. *Anchorage Daily Times*, December 6, 1924.
64. Ibid., January 16, 1925.
65. Ibid., May 26, 1925.
66. *The Alaska Weekly*, March 19, 1926.
67. Ibid., July 30, 1926.
68. Jean Potter. *Alaska Under Arms*, p. 182.
69. *The Alaska Weekly*, April 1, 1927.
70. Ibid., January 27, 1928.
71. *Cordova Daily Times*, May 21, 1928.
72. *Wickersham Diary*, April 12, 1930. UAA Archives microfilm.
73. *Fairbanks Daily News-Miner*, April 11, 1930.
74. Ibid., April 23, 1930.
75. *Anchorage Daily Times*, June 7, 1932.
76. Ibid., May 14, 1932.
77. Jo Anne Wold. "Women in His Life". *Fairbanks Daily News-Miner*, January 28, 1978, B3.
78. *Cordova Daily Times*, January 23, 1932.
79. *Anchorage Daily Times*, July 26, 1932.
80. *Cordova Daily Times*, June 27, 1932.
81. Ibid., October 27, 1932.
82. Ibid., February 25, 1933.
83. *Fairbanks Daily News-Miner*, December 11, 1929.
84. *Cordova Daily Times*, April 26, 1933.
85. Interview with Albert Swalling.
86. *Cordova Daily Times*, May 10, 1933.
87. Ibid., June 14, 1933.
88. Ibid., July 14, 1933.

89. *Anchorage Daily Times*, October 24, 1933.
90. *Cordova Daily Times* November 25, 1933.
91. *Anchorage Daily Times*, March 21, 1934.
92. *Cordova Daily Times*, January 19, 1935.
93. Ibid., February 27, 1935.
94. Ibid., March 26, 1935.
95. Ibid., November 18, 1935.
96. Ibid., April 2, 1936.
97. Ibid., March 24, 1936.
98. Ibid., June 3, 1937.
99. Georg Nelson Meyers. "Alaska's Only Home-Grown Millionaire". *Cosmopolitan*, October 1948, p.114.
100. *Seattle Post-Intelligencer*, May 4, 1939.
101. Interview with Miriam Dickey Kinsey.
102. Charles Barker. "The Man in the Battered Hat". *Alaska Life*, April 1940.
103. Interview with Albert Swalling.
104. Interview with Alvin Bramstedt. 105. Interview with Mrs. Bruce Staser.
106. Georg Nelson Meyers. "Alaska's Only Home-Grown Millionaire". *Cosmopolitan*, October 1948, p.111.
107. Interview with Mr. and Mrs. Austin Cooley.
108. Interview with August Hiebert.
109. Potter. *Alaska Under Arms*, p.129.
110. Meyers. "Alaska's Only Home-Grown Millionaire", p.114.
111. Potter. *Alaska Under Arms*, p.127.
112. Interview with Alvin Bramstedt.
113. Ibid.
114. Barbara Snyder Berry. "Movie Palace by Default". *Alaska Journal*, No.11 (1981), p.3.
115. Ibid., p.2.
116. *Anchorage Daily Times*, June 2, 1947.
117. "Heartland Magazine". *Fairbanks Daily News-Miner*, March 12, 1989.
118. *Fairbanks Daily News-Miner*, August 5, 1947.
119. Ernest Gruening. *Many Battles*, p.283.
120. *Cordova Daily Times*, November 18, 1935.
121. *Fairbanks Daily News-Miner*, December 6, 1939.
122. Ibid., December 8, 1939.
123. *Anchorage Daily Times*, February 15, 1941.
124. Ibid., January 29, 1941.
125. *Fairbanks Daily News-Miner*, March 12, 1941.
126. *Anchorage Daily Times*, April 9, 1941.
127. Ibid., April 17, 1941.
128. Gruening. *Many Battles*, p.301.
129. Claus Naske. "Dr. Alaska: Ernest Gruening". *Interpreting Alaska's History*, p.379.
130. *Anchorage Daily Times*, April 15, 1941.
131. *Fairbanks Daily News-Miner*, March 19, 1946.
132. Ibid., October 7, 1946.
133. Ibid., September 2, 1947.
134. *Anchorage Daily Times*, March 19, 1947.
135. Ibid., March 24, 1947.

136. Ibid., April 4, 1947.
137. Ibid., September 3, 1947.
138. *Fairbanks Daily News-Miner*, September 2, 1947.
139. Ibid., January 12, 1948.
140. Ibid., March 8, 1948.
141. Ibid., March 13, 1948.
142. Ibid., April 27, 1948.
143. Ibid., May 3, 1948.
144. Interview with Robert Atwood.
145. *Anchorage Daily News*, April 13, 1949.
146. *Anchorage Daily Times*, December 18, 1948.
147. Ibid., December 20, 1948.
148. Ibid., March 7, 1949.
149. Gruening. *Many Battles*, p.354.
150. *Anchorage Daily Times*, March 7, 1949.
151. Ibid., March 30, 1949.
152. Gruening. *Many Battles*, p.358.
153. Gruening. *Many Battles*, p.358.
154. Naske. "Dr. Alaska: Ernest Gruening", p.388.
155. *Anchorage Daily Times*, April 2, 1949.
156. Naske. "Dr. Alaska: Ernest Gruening", p.390. 157. *Fairbanks Daily News-Miner* April 1, 1949.
158. *Anchorage Daily News*, July 8, 1949.
159. *The Alaska Weekly*, March 10, 1950.
160. Interviews with August Hiebert and Alvin Bramstedt.
161. Interview with Robert Atwood.
162. *Anchorage Daily Times*, March 6, 1950.
163. Ibid.
164. *Fairbanks Daily News-Miner*, March 31, 1950.
165. *Anchorage Daily Times*, June 6, 1950.
166. Ibid., June 10, 1950.
167. *Fairbanks Daily News-Miner*, June 17, 1950.
168. *Anchorage Daily Times*, April 27, 1950.
169. Ibid., May 19, 1950.
170. Taped interview with Austin Lathrop provided by Miriam Dickey Kinsey.
171. *Fairbanks Daily News-Miner*, July 26, 1950.
172. Ibid., July 31, 1950.
173. *Anchorage Daily Times*, August 17, 1950.
174. *The Alaska Weekly*, November 9, 1951.
175. *Fairbanks Daily News-Miner*, October 31, 1951.
176. Gruening. *Many Battles*, p.383.
177. Ibid., p.381.
178. Ibid., p.389.
179. Interview with Robert Atwood.
180. Interview with Mrs. August Hiebert.
181. *Anchorage Daily Times*, April 3, 1958.
182. Gruening. *Many Battles*, p.389.

BIBLIOGRAPHY

Banks, Della Murray "A Game of Bluff" in *Alaska Sportsman*, Oct. 1945.

"Hope Springs Eternal" *Alaska Sportsman*, Jan. 1946.

Barker, Charles "The Man and the Battered Hat" in *Alaska Life*, Apr. 1940.

Buzzell, Rolfe "Mining in the Burning Hills" Unpublished manuscript.

Ferber, Edna *Ice Palace* . New York: Doubleday & Co., 1958.

Glenn, Capt. Edwin F. *Reports of Explorations in the Territory of Alaska, 1898*, Washington D.C.: Govt. Printing Office, 1899.

Gruening, Ernest *Many Battles* New York: Liveright, 1973.

Hearst, Joseph "Alaskan Midas" in *Chicago Sunday Tribune Graphic Magazine*, August 8, 1948.

Koman, John *Alaska's Turnagain Arm*, Anchorage: Ram Publications, 1989.

Laird, Paul "Austin E. 'Cap' Lathrop" in *Alaska Business Monthly*, Jan. 1988.

McClain, Chris "Austin 'Cap' Lathrop in *Greatlander*, October 13, 1971.

Meyers, Georg Nelson "Alaska's Only Homegrown Millionaire" in *Cosmopolitan*. Oct. 1948.

Morgan, A.W. *Memories of Old Sunrise,* Anchorage: Cook Inlet Historical Society, 1994.

Naske, Claus-M "Dr. Alaska: Ernest Gruening" in *Interpreting Alaska's History* (Anchorage: APU Press, 1989).

Potter, Jean *Alaska Under Arms*, New York: The MacMillan Company, 1942.

Ray, Joan Alita "Cap Lathrop" in *Alaskana*, Dec. 1971.

Solka, Paul *Adventures in Alaska Journalism,* Fairbanks: Commercial Printing Co.,1980.

Wold, Jo Anne "A Matter of Timing" in *Fairbanks News-Miner*, Jan. 14,1979.

"Win and Lose" in *Fairbanks News-Miner*, Jan. 21, 1979.

"Women in His Life" in *Fairbanks News-Miner*, Jan. 28, 1979.

"The Man" in *Fairbanks New-Miner*, Feb. 4, 1979.

"Miriam Speaks" in *Fairbanks News-Miner*, Feb. 11, 1979.

Index

Abercrombie Rapids 57
Admiral Schley 48
Alaska Airlines 101
Alaska Coast Company 34
Alaska Commercial Co. 11, 12, 14, 16
Alaska Labor Union 46,
Alaska Life 82, 122, 124
Alaska Motion Picture Corp. 50
Alaska Railroad
  39, 49, 50, 57, 62, 65, 86, 111
Alaska Steamship Co. 68, 108
Alaska Syndicate 27, 38, 68
Alaskatalla Petroleum Co. 49
Alaska Transfer Co. 28, 30, 33, 35
Alaska Yukon Magazine 32
An American Citizen 42
American Lifograph Co. 50, 51
Anacortes Railroad 9
Anacortes, Washington 8, 9, 10, 40
Anchorage Chamber of Commerce 50
Anchorage Daily News 103, 123
Anchorage Democrat 47
Anchorage-Willow Creek Mining
and Development Company 45
Arctic Lumber Company 30
Arnold, W.C. 85, 100, 110
Ashland, Wisconsin 8
Atwood, Robert B. 3, 100, 103, 115, 123
Baker, L.W. 113
Bank of Anchorage 45, 46
Barrymore, John 42
Banks, Della 13, 14, 15, 120
Bartlett Glacier 54,
Bell, Joe 26, 27
Bennett, Stanton 84, 85
Bertha 32, 22
Billie Burke 42
Bird Creek 13
Bonanza Mine 27, 28
Boyce, Mrs. J.A. 29
Bramstedt, Al 3, 88, 89, 114, 122, 123
Brown, Norman 103
Burton, Richard 5, 119
California-Alaska Mining
Development Co. 26, 27
Canby 13, 14
Captain Durfee 14
Captain Kelly 11, 15, 78
Castner, Lieut. J C 17, 18
Cheechako 57
Chicago Tribune 37, 38, 61, 120
Childs Glacier 57, 58
Chilkoot Pass 54
Clara Nevada 15
Clawson, John H. 71, 72, 73, 90

Cleary Creek 70
Coffey, Edward W. 90
Coal Bay 21, 62
Conklin and Fitzgerald 42
Cook Inlet
    11-14, 16,18, 20-23, 40, 57, 124
Cook Inlet Pioneer 40
Cooley, Austin 3, 84, 85, 113, 122
Coolidge, President Calvin 61
Copper River and Northwestern
    Railroad 33, 38, 68, 70, 71, 77
Copper River Railroad 25, 26
Cordova
    26-39, 41, 43, 47-51, 55-58,
    65-68, 70-78, 84, 110, 112-114
Cordova Air Service 75
Cordova Chamber of Commerce
    35, 71, 73
Cordova Coal Party 32, 33, 34
Cordova Daily Alaskan
    28-30, 32-34, 36, 39, 120
Cordova Orchestra 37
Corlew, G.D. 23
Cosmopolitan 84, 122, 124
Costello, J.H. 23, 24, 25
Costello Oil Land Co. 25
Crane, Rev. D.W. 21
Daily Alaska Empire 101, 109
DeGraff, Ruby 35, 47, 48, 65, 70
Dickey, Miriam
    3, 70, 71, 79, 113, 122, 123
Dry Bay 23
Duncan, Ray 81
Dyea 12
Egan, William 115
Eisenhower, Gen Dewight D. 93, 114
Elsner, Senator Richard 48
Empress Theater, Anchorage 40, 48, 92
Empress Theater, Cordova 36-38, 72

Empress Theater, Fairbanks
    67, 101, 111, 111
Empress Theatre, Valdez 41
Ervin, E. Wells 90, 92
Evan Jones Coal Co. 108, 110
Excelsior 23, 24
Eyak Lake 57
Fairbanks 66, 78-85, 93
Fairbanks Exploration Co. 66, 82, 83
Fairbanks Golf Club 93
Fairbanks News Miner 67, 78, 107, 114
Ferber, Edna 5, 115, 117, 118, 124
First Bank of Cordova 34, 71, 72, 74
Fourth Avenue Theater
    5, 86, 89, 92, 103, 119
Galen, James L. 71, 72
Gelineau, J.R 26, 27
Gillam Airways 75
Girdwood 13, 52, 53
Glacier Packing Co. 75, 76
Glacier Sea Foods 76, 77
Glenn, Captain E.E. 16-20, 120
Glenn Expedition 17
Gordon, Eva 57, 64
Gottstein, J.B. 107
Gruening, Ernest
    96-109. 115, 118, 122-124
Guggenheim-Morgan Alaska
    Syndicate 27
Harding, President Warren 57, 63
Harrison, President Benjamin 30
Harsh, Albert 97
Harwood, E.J 36
Hazelet, George 68
Healy River Coal Mines Corp.
    64, 70, 82, 86, 87, 110, 114
Heinzelman, Frank 115
Heney, M.J. 25, 26
Hewitt, A.J. 70

Hewitt, D.E.   90
Hiebert, August 3, 84, 85, 114, 122, 123
Hill, Harry   90, 103, 113
Hineberg Decorating Co.   90
Hollywood   51, 58, 59
Hope   13, 14
Hughes, Charles Evans   43
Ice Palace
    4, 5, 114,115, 117, 118, 119, 124
Ivey, J.W.   23
Jefferson, Joseph   81
Jones, Charles D.   105
Juneau
    11, 43, 48, 49, 57, 73, 95, 96, 100,
107-109
Kanatak   63
Katalla   12, 23, 27, 49
Katalla Herald   27
Kelly, Captain   11, 15
KENI   103. 106, 119
Kennicott Glacier   27
Ketchikan   43, 104, 107
KFAR   4, 78, 80, 81,84-88, 93, 106
Kimball Pipe Organ   44, 45, 66
Knik Arm   17, 18
Knik Station   18
Kodiak   11, 12, 21
Kotsina River   26
L.J. Perry   4, 11, 15, 17, 21, 23
Lacey Street Theater 5, 81-83, 86, 119
Ladds Station   16, 18
Lake Becharof   21, 25
Lakme   12
Lathrop Building, Anchorage
                      40, 41, 45, 64, 65
Lathrop Building, Cordova 74, 78, 81
Lathrop Building, Fairbanks 78, 80, 89
Lathrop Company   5, 75, 112
Latouche   48

Laurence, Sidney   47, 58
Lee, Jack   21, 25
Lewis, George Edward 50, 51, 55, 60
Libby, T. J.   12
Los Angeles Sunday Times   57
Many Battles   118, 122-124
Marquam, Thomas   68
McCutcheon, Stanley   99, 104
McDonald, A.B.   50, 51, 60
McDowell, Miss Cleo   21-23
McDowell, Mrs. Lillian   21-23
McKinley Park Tourist and
Transportation Co.   71
McKinley, President Wm.   23
Medley, Edward F.   113
Meyers, George Nelson 84, 122, 124
Midnight Sun Broadcasting Co. 80, 81
Moomaw, L.H   51, 52, 60
Mt. McKinley   53, 59, 90
Mt. McKinley National Park 47, 52, 71
National Bank of Alaska   45, 69
National Recovery Act   73
Nenana   50, 56, 88
Nerland, A. Leslie   111
New York City   60, 85
Ninilchik   13
Nome   43, 96, 100, 105
Nome City   24
O'Brien, Captain Johnny   13
O'Neil, John   11, 15
Olympia Beer   83
Olympia Brewing Company   34, 83
Pacific Alaska Navigation Company 34
Pan American Expedition   23
Parks, George   69
Pathe-Hearst   44
Pathe-International Film Co.   60, 63
Paul, William   69
Pfaud, Southall   81

Porreca, A.A. 89
Portage Glacier 13
Portland, Oregon
34, 50, 51, 59, 65, 73, 110
Prince William Sound 13, 22, 23, 38
Priteca, Marcus 89
Purvis, George B. 47, 66
Rasmuson, Edward A. 69, 71, 103, 108
Raynor, Sydney C. 113, 114
Republican National Convention 68
Republican Party 10, 48, 67, 108
Rivers, Ralph 115
Roosevelt, President Franklin 69, 72, 95
Rustgard, John 69
San Francisco 30, 31
Schechert, Miss Marquerite 52
Schmidt, Leopold 34
Schmidt, Peter 83
Seattle
8, 10, 11, 15, 21-24,26, 29, 31, 37,
39, 43, 47, 48, 56, 59, 65, 70-73, 76,
78, 80, 83, 86, 95, 107, 112, 122
Seattle Post-Intelligencer 80, 122
Seward 41, 43, 50, 51, 65, 120
Sherman Anti Trust 108
Ship Creek 39, 40
Smith, Tom 12
Standard Oil 62, 63
Stella Erland 16
Stevens, Ed 87, 88
Stone, Bernard, M. 69
Strand, William C. 107, 114
Sundberg, George 101
Sunrise 13-16, 18, 20,120, 124
Suntrana 67, 70, 84, 86, 112
Susitna Valley 39
Tanana Publishing Co., Inc. 67
Territorial Legislature 48, 97, 100
The Alaska Prospector 23, 25, 120

The Alaska Times 35, 38
The Alaska Weekly
57, 65, 66, 70, 76, 121, 123
The Cheechako 3, 52-56, 58-61, 63-65
The Jolson Story 92
The Valdez News 22-24, 26, 120
Thompson, W.F. 56, 67
Troy, John W. 95
Truman, President Harry 101-103
Turnagain Arm 12-15, 17, 52
Tyonek 14
University of Alaska 69, 101, 113
Usibelli Coal Co 108
Utopia 13
Vigna, Pietro 81
Walker, Norman 99
Western Alaska Fair 61
White House 61
White Pass and Yukon Route 26
Wickersham, James 43, 68,69, 121
Williams, L.L. 22
Wilson, President Woodrow 39, 63
World War II 5, 85, 86, 98
Zeigler, A.H. 104
Ziegler, Eustace 28, 90